The Aspiring Traveler's Handbook

A preparation guide to international travel

by Jackie Nourse Laulainen
of The Budget-Minded Traveler Blog

The Aspiring Traveler's Handbook: A preparation guide to international travel.

First Edition.

The information in this book is not guaranteed to be up-to-date, nor should it be understood as the only correct way to accomplish international travel.

There are many references to Third Parties in this book, none of which guarantee the performance or effectiveness of their products or services. All references are merely recommendations based on the author's own experiences. As such, the author assumes no responsibility or liability for any Third Party material, products, services, or opinions.

Any names of people in this book have either been changed for privacy or used with permission.

Cover design, photos, and interior design by Jackie Laulainen. Author photo and content artwork by Sabrina Schreibeis.

By reading this book, you agree that the author is not responsible for the outcome, whether successful or not, of the decisions you make regarding traveling abroad.

For more information, visit www.TheBudgetMindedTraveler.com.

This book is dedicated to my parents. Thank you for encouraging me to travel the world, for being my biggest fans and for making me believe that I can do anything, even publish a book.

To all of my friends who have ever and will ever come to me for travel advice, you are my inspiration! Thank you for taking me on this journey.

About the Author

My name is Jackie Laulainen, and I have been bitten by the almighty Travel Bug.

Since 2003, I have spent a good part of my life living, studying, or traveling abroad. My most extensively-traveled areas of the world are Latin America and Europe, both of which are very popular destinations for American travelers. As a result of my experiences, I have become more and more of a resource for all things travel. My knack for traveling on a budget is nothing less than mind-boggling for most people, and this tends to be a popular subject among aspiring travelers.

I have created a website called The Budget-Minded Traveler, which you can find online at www.thebudgetmindedtraveler.com. The website is an interactive platform that goes hand-in-hand with this book and also includes a blog and many helpful travel resources. The website, the book, and The Budget-Minded Traveler on social media are my avenues of connecting and sharing with those who want to learn the tricks of the travel trade, especially on a budget. Travel is truly my passion. I find (and share) ways to make it happen, and I hope I can inspire you to discover it for yourself.

Table of Contents

Introduction 1

Chapter 1: Deciding Where To Go..7
  Research Your Destination Country 8
  Where To Find All This Information 12
  Affording Your Trip 13
  Some Travel Logistics To Consider 15
  Getting A Passport..17

Chapter 2: Planning Your Flight...19
  Actively Search Several Websites...................................19
  Research The Best Days To Book *And* Travel....................21
  Benefits Of One-Way And Round-The-World Tickets..........24
  Be Creative With Airports..25
  Plan For Changes You Don't Know You Might Need 27

Chapter 3: Budgeting 31
  Budget Accommodations 32
    Couch Surfing 37
    Working And Volunteering Abroad 40
  Budget Transportation 42
    A Note About German Trains 43
    Cheap Flights Throughout Europe 43
  Student Discounts 45
  Budget Eating 46

Chapter 4: Packing: Less Is More......................................51
  What Does Your Luggage Look Like?................................51
    Three Things To Look For In A Good Backpack 52
    Where Do You Get A Good Backpack?.......................54
    Three Things To Look For In A Good Suitcase 55
  What To Put In Your Luggage 56
    Packing It All Up 61

Avoid Checking Bags If Possible...63

Chapter 5: Leaving It All Behind 66
What To Do With Your US Cell Phone Account 67
What To Do With Your Stuff...68
Staying On Top Of Your Bills...69
Financial Matters At Home..70

Chapter 6: Being Safety-Smart 72
Keep Your Luggage In Sight 74
The Trick About Zippers And Safety Pins..............................76
Keep Inventory Of Your Valuables...78
Don't Fall Victim To The Tourist Trap 81
Alcohol And Safety 85
Women Traveling Alone 86

Chapter 7: Getting Money Abroad 89
Bringing US Cash...90
Using Your ATM Card 90
Using Your Credit Card 91
Getting Foreign Currency From Your Bank............................92
Contact Your Banks 92
Have A Backup Plan...93

Chapter 8: Making It Work Abroad 95
Cell Phones..95
How To Get A SIM Card Abroad 97
Must-Have Travel Apps 98
Visa Issues 102
Travel Insurance 103
What To Look For In Travel Insurance Coverage 104
Adapters And Converters 107

Chapter 9: Study Abroad..109

Conclusion...113

Thank You! 115

Introduction

August 2003: With an overwhelming anticipation I had never known before, I sat glued to the window as my flight descended over the beautiful, green mountains of Costa Rica. I remember suddenly realizing that this foreign country, in which I was about to set foot for the first time, was going to be my home for the next  academic year. I may have been 18 years old and in college at the time, but what I didn't realize is that my life was really just about to begin. There is no way I could have predicted how much that single trip would change my life and open my eyes to the world and at the same time teach me more and more about myself with each passing day.

That was ten years ago, when the "Travel Bug" officially bit me. I have been subject to its powers ever since. *There is a freedom and ever-expanding horizon that comes with traveling the world that I am simply addicted to exploring, and the journey has taught me more than a classroom ever could.*

Compared to the average American, I have spent an abnormal amount of time abroad in the last ten years. I have studied abroad three times, I have been to over 35 countries (and counting) outside of the US, and I don't plan to change this pattern any time soon. I even managed to get married and adopt a dog along the way, but did  that change my passion for travel? No way, it's ingrained in me. Once the Travel Bug bites, there is no turning back. At least there isn't for me.

Words can only attempt to describe what comes from an experience of traveling or studying abroad. The bottom line is that it demands to be experienced first-hand to be truly understood. I will tell you now that if you travel abroad, you will grow as a person more than you knew you could. I will also tell you that you will test yourself in ways you haven't before, you will learn about people of a different culture, you will gain confidence you didn't know you had and at the same time learn about your weaknesses. You will finally learn about what your *own* culture looks like from the *out*side. I am happy to tell you all these things and more, but until you go experience it for yourself, you will just have to take my word for it. *My goal in writing this book is to equip you*

2

with tools and tips that you can use when you go abroad, but the "going" part is up to you. What exactly are the experiences that will test you, teach you, enlighten you, change you, move you, and leave you wanting more? You can read as many articles and books as you want, but no one can answer that question except you.

I have found that a lot of people who have never traveled before (and I used to be the same way) often have so many questions that they don't even know what their questions are. Because of my extensive traveling over the years to destinations popular among Americans, a lot of these people in my life have come to me for travel advice. I get questions like: How much is this going to cost? How do I find a good flight? Where do I look for  hostels? Should I get a backpack? Do I need a visa? How do I go about getting a visa? Do I need immunizations? I don't even have a passport yet! What…? Where…? Who…? The list goes on and on.

You can probably see from the size of this book that travel advice is not something I take lightly. In fact, I have probably inundated my friends with so much travel advice that they couldn't possibly keep it all in their heads. All the while, I know that there is so much more information they could benefit from than simply what we can cover over a cup of coffee, a phone call, or an email. As a result, I've made an effort to put it all into one place, answering as many questions as I can, based on my own experiences. I'm not claiming to know  everything there is to know about travel, but I am aiming to equip you with what I do know. There is a lot of information in this book, so if you are not the note-taking kind (or even if you are), you may be happy to learn that you can find most of the resources mentioned in this book and much more information on my website at www.thebudgetmindedtraveler.com.

My hope is that this book will be a step-by-step guide to helping you make that first trip a reality. Some parts are geared more towards the long-term, budget traveler, but most of the information can be beneficial to any type of international traveler. It is a compilation of many of the tricks of the travel trade that I have learned in the last ten years, from buying a plane ticket, to staying on a budget, to keeping thieves out of your luggage. It is inspired by eager and aspiring travelers and written for the many who could label themselves the same.

My mission is to inspire and prepare those of you who want (or wish) to travel to actually get out your doors and do it. My challenge to you is that you put what you learn from reading this book to use and go meet the world and the "you" that is waiting to be discovered. May you find the inspiration and education you need to introduce yourself to the world of travel, and may you, like many travelers before you, never be the same.

Throughout this book, keep an eye out for these little guys who will point out some good stuff!

The Travel Bug   The Budget Bug

Chapter 1: Deciding Where To Go

Before you start planning any other part of your trip, there is one very obvious and important question you need to know: where are you going? You might already have an idea of a foreign country or group of countries that you would like to visit; you may even know which airport you need to fly into and out of; on the other hand, you may not. There are a few things to consider while planning where to travel. For example:

- What is the foreign country's current civil state?

- How much money will you need?

- Do you need a visa?

- Do you need vaccinations?

- Will it be possible to see and do all you want to see and do in the time you have allocated?

- Are you prepared for a language barrier?

- What will the weather be like when and where you will be traveling?

These questions may seem a bit overwhelming to you now, but we will work through them together in this chapter!

Research Your Destination Country

Most people have not just one but usually a whole list of countries they would like to visit "one day." That list is the perfect place to start. If you are flexible with the time of year that you are able to travel, then your number one destination should be your first answer, followed by a couple of backup plans should you run into any problems with your first destination. If you are short on time or only have a certain allotted couple of weeks or months to travel, then it would do you well to keep in mind what time of year that will be, and my point here is that weather matters!

For example, if you are planning an amazing beach vacation to Costa Rica, then I hope you are going between January and April so as to not get caught in the rainy season. On the other hand, accommodation prices are lower in the off-season and you still get some sun in those rainy months, but never is that sunshine guaranteed like it is in the dry months. If you want a perfect beach getaway to the Caribbean, you might want to make sure it's not hurricane season. If you are trying to go to the Greek Islands, I would recommend going before the end of September when many places close down for the "stormy season." You get the picture, right? The bottom line is to know what to expect. Do a bit of research and pick a place that coincides well with the season that you are allotting for your trip.

The next three steps can be done in any order, but they are all equally important:

1. Check on the country's current civil state.

Why is this important? If you have your heart set on Thailand, and suddenly a civil war breaks out in Bangkok, you may want to reconsider. If your destination country is having any sort of civil unrest, natural disaster or otherwise, you could be unnecessarily putting yourself in danger simply by inserting yourself into the equation.

2. Find out if you need to apply for a visa.

Many countries require a visa for entry, and this requirement varies depending on your nationality. There are two ways to acquire visas:

- prior to your trip altogether, or

- "on arrival" when you arrive at immigration in that country, either by plane or border crossing.

A "Visa On Arrival" is the most common. Sometimes this is simply issued by a stamp in your passport as you pass through immigration, and sometimes you actually need to pay for it when you cross a land border or land in an airport in that country. Unless your destination country requires you to get a visa before you come, all you need to do is show up, and you will be told what to do as you go through immigration. A Visa on Arrival does not often require any special documentation. However, you may need to prove onward travel (that you do not plan to stay in that country for too long), or that you have had certain vaccinations, etc. A Visa On Arrival is usually easy to get, and will sometimes cost money depending on the country.

What you really need to be aware of are the countries that require you to take care of acquiring a visa *before* you travel. Depending on where you live and what region your town or city falls under in terms of consulates, you may be required to travel to another US city for your visa appointment. There is no way around this, so just be sure to plan ahead to allow yourself plenty of time to make the trip.

 *"What you really need to be aware of are the countries that require you to take care of acquiring a visa **before** you travel."*

One country that has such requirements, for US citizens traveling from the US, is Brazil. Without your visa in-hand, US airport employees may not even allow you to check in for your flight to Brazil, and if you end up in Brazil without proper documentation, there is nothing the US government can do to help you. If you are flying from the US to a country with rules like Brazil, don't wait until it's too late! Look it up *online* on an up-to-date website before you go. Here's another tip: if immigration officers give you a stamped form or note separate from your passport stamp on arrival, make sure you keep it. Sometimes you need these stamped forms to get out of the country.

3. Find out if you need any specific vaccinations.

This cannot be disregarded as unimportant, and I personally cannot stress this enough. Can you tell I have learned the hard way? I will save that story for another day. If the country you are traveling to *requires* any vaccinations, be sure to make an appointment with a travel vaccination clinic in your area well ahead of time. I will get more into those in a minute. Some vaccinations are administered in sequences and take more than one visit to complete. Most importantly, DO NOT LOSE your yellow international vaccination card that you will be given by your vaccine administrator. This card details which vaccines you have received and the dates they were administered to you. Without it, well, let's just say I've been there, and it's really not a place you want to find yourself when rules are strict.

Where To Find All This Information

I highly recommend checking out these two websites for up-to-date information about your destination country:

- **www.travel.state.gov** – This website, managed by the Bureau of Consular Affairs of the US Department of State, is a very resourceful site where you can find *country-specific, up-to-date information about visa requirements (including consular jurisdiction), safety threats and crime, as well as insurance, passport help, and so on.*

- **www.cdc.gov/travel** – The Center for Disease Control and Prevention website describes in detail *which (if any) current vaccinations are required to enter your selected country, which vaccinations are recommended for that country, what diseases could be a possible threat in that country, and where you can find a travel clinic to administer these vaccines to you.*

Thoroughly researching the visa and vaccination requirements, news, and safety tips for your specific country can save you a lot of stress later. Check more than one source as well, because although your Lonely Planet guidebook may be the most recent edition published, it may not reflect the same information that the most up-to-date website could provide for you (and they are the first to warn you of this!). Trust me on this one.

 "...your Lonely Planet guidebook... may not reflect the same information that the most up-to-date website could provide for you..."

The reason I recommend reading the news and checking these websites for information about your destination country is to make sure that there isn't a civil war going on or new visa requirements that you aren't aware of that could affect your travel plans, to say the least. If parts of Mexico are becoming dangerous due to drug trafficking, you may want to avoid those places; likewise, if terrorist threats are high in London or Paris as they have been in the past, perhaps that shouldn't be your first choice. If Ecuador just had an attempted coup, maybe it wouldn't be the wisest to travel there. Even if your guidebook says one thing about visas, double-check the information online, because rules can change every day. These very real examples are not meant to deter you from traveling. Rather, they are simply meant to make you a smart traveler who is aware of what you are getting into before you buy your plane ticket.

Affording Your Trip

Another very important issue to consider that might help you decide where you should go is your financial situation. I will get more into budgeting in Chapter 3, but what I'm referring to here is how much it will cost you to be in your selected country for an extended period of time. It is a good idea to check the currency exchange rate before taking off. Keep in mind that if you're heading to Europe, especially the UK, the US Dollar has been very weak (meaning it doesn't get you very far) against their Euros and Pounds in recent years. On the other hand, there are many countries where a dollar will go a long way, and you could conceivably go to these places for twice the time and half the money that it would cost to go to a more expensive country.

If you purchase a guidebook for the specific area or country of your choice, often times you will find an estimated per diem cost of living for that country. You can always look this up online as well. This will give you a rough idea of how much you might spend each day, and then of course you need to factor in the costs of any special activities that you plan to do. I prefer the Lonely Planet guidebooks, but I know there are many excellent resources in print if you just take the time to look for them. That being said, I must insert disclaimer here about guidebooks: do not depend solely on guidebooks! The information in them is never guaranteed as the most up-to-date and accurate, as they cannot keep up with the constant changes made everyday in countries across the world. However, they prove to be a great place to start to get to know your destination country.

The bottom line about money is to be aware of what it will cost you to pay for food, accommodations, and activities on your trip. Make sure you can afford to go where you're going. If your budget is really limited, you have a decision to make about whether to go to London for one week or Guatemala for three!

Some Travel Logistics To Consider

There are always some simpler logistics to consider when deciding where to travel. Two of these examples that I mentioned were the possibility of a language barrier and whether or not you are realistically giving yourself enough time to cover the ground you expect to cover and see the sites that you want to see.

I brought up the language barrier because I happen to be a linguist and a firm believer that Americans should make an attempt to communicate with other citizens of the world in a language other than English. It is true that English is the worldwide common language, but that doesn't mean that we can't have a bit of fun trying to learn some phrases that will help us out on the road! I find that most people truly appreciate any attempt that I make to speak their language. Equally, most people who have even a little knowledge of English will be eager to speak it with you, which, in turn, makes your life easier if foreign language is not your forte.

Don't count on rumors you hear that English is spoken everywhere, as it really and truly is *not* spoken everywhere. If you are setting yourself up for a visit with a language barrier, be prepared. Bring along a phrasebook, learn some local pronunciation, and give it your best shot. In most cases, you really will be able to use English, but be aware that it won't always work.

Language barriers are just one of the many reasons traveling is an adventure.

As for your time allocation, try to be realistic. If you know you can make it through all the museums in Paris in one week, good for you. However, if you turn out to be one of those people who could spend five entire days just going through the many rooms of the Louvre alone, then don't just give yourself one week in Paris if you want to see it all! You will miss out on so much, and you came all this way…. If you think two weeks is enough time to do five countries in Europe, you are right. However, it might include traveling on overnight trains more than you wanted to and probably losing sleep, which then makes you too tired to run with the bulls!

If you think you can make it from Mexico to Colombia in two months *and* see everything in between, you are setting yourself up for disappointment! You'd have to skip a country or two, and then you will not have seen everything. Do you KNOW how amazing Guatemala is? And did you know that you can't even take a bus over land from Panama to Colombia? You need to fly or take a boat, which can take several days just to arrange. Be prepared for realities! You might fall in love with Guatemala and spend so much time there that you completely skip Costa Rica, which I would not recommend. Perhaps you are planning a trip to Australia. If you plan to visit all sides of the country then I hope you plan to fly. Australia is HUGE, so make sure you have enough time and that your bank account is big enough to cover the extra flights.

Whatever your plans entail, try not to be over ambitious to the point where you can't remember all the places you visited or the names of any of the people you met, or what exactly was going on in that photo, because these are the things that make the memories of traveling special. Any way you make it happen, I can almost guarantee that it will leave you yearning for more. You'll just have to go back "one day."

Getting A Passport

If you do not yet possess a passport, you will need one to leave the country and this should be one of your first orders of business if you are planning a trip abroad. If you are applying for a US passport for the first time, you must apply in person. This can be done at one of your local post offices. Not all post offices have passport agents, so before you go driving all over town, get online and find out which one near you provides passport services. Keep in mind there are several things you will need to take with you to apply for a US passport, and they can all be found on the previously-mentioned website Travel.state.gov:

- Form DS-11: Application for US Passport; remember *not* to sign it until instructed to do so by the agent;

- Evidence of US citizenship: A birth certificate or the like;

- Identification *and* a copy of it as well;

- One passport photo;

- A check for the appropriate amount (this amount will be posted online);

Depending on how busy the passport issuing centers are at the moment, it can take anywhere from 3-6 weeks to get your passport. This processing time is updated periodically and can be found online in order to help you plan accordingly.

If you need to renew or change your current passport, you can do this via US mail. You will need to fill out Form DS-82: Application for US Passport by Mail, and provide the appropriate documentation. A note to those renewing or changing names on passports: yes, you must submit your old passport (I know, it's hard) for processing, but no, they don't keep it. Your old passport and any accompanying documentation you submitted *will* be sent back to you, in a separate mailing from your new passport.

Once you've applied for your passport and made a decision about just the right place and time to go, you know what comes next: buying a plane ticket!

Chapter 2: Planning Your Flight

You may not be aware of this, but there are several pieces to the puzzle of putting together a flight itinerary and even some strategy involved. For example, did you know that you could possibly save money by creating a multi-leg itinerary rather than a single-destination, round-trip flight? Did you know that there are certain times of day and even days of the week that are better to BUY your ticket than others? Do you know which days are cheapest to fly on? Did you know that some search engines are generally cheaper than others? I'm going to assume you answered "no" to at least one of these questions, and that is where I come in to help you figure it out.

Actively Search Several Websites

One of the biggest obstacles to get over when planning a trip is purchasing your airline ticket. Everyone wants a deal, no one wants to find out they paid way too much for a ticket, and there is just something about committing to that "purchase" button that fills people with anxiety. Many novice travelers don't know where to start, how to go about looking for their ticket, how much they should expect to pay, and whether they should book a one-way, round-trip, or even multi-city flight. This chapter is meant to help you sort out this dilemma.

Here is one of my favorite travel tool tips: look into multi-city itineraries if it might be convenient for your plans. It is not always the case, but if you would like to cover a lot of ground, a multi-destination itinerary could end up being the most economic option even if the price is a bit higher than a regular round-trip fare. From the list provided below, Skyscanner.com is the only site (at time of publishing) that does not support multi-city travel, but it tends to have cheaper deals on round-trip fares, so it is still one of my top choices. Here is a list of my favorite flight search engines in no particular order:

- www.skyscanner.com

- www.airfare.com

- www.cheaptickets.com

- www.cheapoair.com

- www.vayama.com

- www.kayak.com

- www.expedia.com

- www.orbitz.com

If you want to find the cheapest fare, you need to *actively* research and compare several sites. I tend to go through phases with each website. I find that one of these websites will be cheaper than all the others for a few months running, and then it will change and one of the others will be cheapest for a turn.

Finding the best deal takes time and patience. This is why I say you need to *actively* research your flight options. In most cases you will not buy your flight the first time you search. You will, however, get an idea of how much it will cost, and you'll automatically have a goal: to find a ticket cheaper than that!

Research The Best Days To Book *And* Travel

I recommend you do a quick online search to find a current report about which days of the week and times of day are best to *buy* your ticket, because it can change a lot over the years. As of when this book was published, most articles will tell you that early midweek is the best time to buy. Airlines tend to put sales out on Mondays, and then by Tuesdays other airlines are competitively lowering their prices. This generally means that Tuesdays and Wednesdays are the best days to buy, because as the week goes on, the sales go away, and the prices go up. Weekends (Saturdays and Sundays) are the most expensive days to buy. Think about it, weekends are the days when most people have the time to think about vacations and search for flights, not knowing that they are falling right into the airlines' traps and buying the most expensive fares. If you see prices go up over the weekend, don't panic and most of all DO NOT fall for it, wait for Tuesday or Wednesday to come back around before you buy.

"If you see prices go up over the weekend, don't panic and most of all DO NOT fall for it, wait for Tuesday or Wednesday to come back around before you buy."

Not only are there cheap days to buy, but there are also cheap days to travel. Booking your flight to depart and return on a Tuesday, Wednesday, or Thursday could save you more money than if you were to travel on a weekend, when it's convenient for everyone else to travel. It tends to be less expensive to travel for 1-3 weeks, which is not necessarily very long for a backpacking trip. Just be aware that once you pass that 30-day mark, your ticket will most likely be more expensive, there's no way around that. Either way, if you do some comparisons you will see that more often than not it is cheaper to fly midweek than on weekends. However, try every combination just in case, as I have found this is the most commonly broken rule.

It is also a good idea to start your searches early so you have plenty of time to find the best deal. You definitely want to have your flight booked at least 14-21 days in advance, but generally 2-3 months in advance is better. Don't fret if you are 5-6 months in advance and prices are sky high, this is normal. Have patience and wait until prices come down. It's not necessarily advantageous to book too far in advance, although you may just get lucky and find a good deal (but that means you have to have an idea of what a good deal is). I once found an amazing round-trip fare from Bozeman, MT (my tiny and expensive home airport) to Berlin, Germany (exactly where we wanted to go) four months in advance for $740, which I certainly did buy that very day knowing that this was an exception because that price was next to impossible. That was my first experience with Airfare.com and I have loved it ever since.

Keep in mind that certain times of year are more expensive to travel than others. For example, summer months (June-August) are considered high season for flying and prices automatically go up because this is when most Americans want to go on vacation. Christmas is, of course, one of the most expensive weeks of the year to travel, unless you travel on Christmas Day. Try to avoid busy times, not just for cheaper prices, but for less crowded airports! Don't forget that other countries have different holidays. It's a good idea to be aware of what might be going on in your destination country when you get there. For example, try going to Latin America during Semana Santa, Munich during Oktoberfest, Rio de Janeiro during Carnaval... you get the picture. You wondered why your flight was so expensive and there were no cheap hotels? It's because everyone else was booking the same flight and hotel room! If your goal happens to be visiting those countries specifically for those holidays, then good luck and be prepared to pay more.

Do a bit of research on the seasons in your destination country. For example, traveling to Costa Rica is cheaper in May-November because it's low season there (which means lots of rain). Hotels and flights will generally be cheaper than they are from December-April, which are the sunny and dry months to visit. If you're traveling to Europe, September could be a great time to go because it's the end of tourist season. Prices are dropping, yet the weather is still nice. Italy almost closes down in August because it's literally vacation month for the whole country. These are just a couple examples of how doing a bit of research could help you know what you are getting into.

Benefits Of One-Way And Round-The-World Tickets

You always have the option to buy a one-way ticket and figure out how to get home later. This can be a great way to leave your trip open-ended and be able to "go where the wind takes you." Just keep in mind that if you find yourself entering a country that requires you to get a visa, you may be asked to show proof of onward travel (that you'll be leaving that country within a certain time period so as to not exceed your visa). If you do not have this, you may be forced to get it before immigration lets you in. You can read more about this in Chapter 8. Buying two one-ways can end up being much more expensive than a round-trip ticket, but it can be beneficial if you really don't know where you'll end up.

Just make sure you have enough money left at the end of your travels to foot the bill for that flight home.

If you plan to be gone for months and think you're going to make it pretty far, it could even be cheaper, yes I said cheaper, to invest in a Round-the-World (RTW) ticket. RTW tickets come in all shapes and sizes and can be a good deal if you know basically where you want to go. Start by doing an online search for round the world tickets, and you should find a surplus of information and websites to help you. In 2009 I bought a one-way ticket to Rome, Italy. Six months later I ended up flying home on a one-way ticket from Istanbul, Turkey, a total of which cost me about $1,200. That's not bad considering it catered to exactly what I needed, and I couldn't possibly have told you that I would be flying home from Istanbul when I originally booked my flight to Italy ten months earlier. However, for another $800 or less I could have continued east and flown all the way around the world... That is, if only my money would have lasted.

If you look at the big picture, that's a great deal compared to my individual searches to find one-way flights from Turkey to India, to Thailand, etc., to get back to the US. RTW can be done and it doesn't have to be too expensive, people do it all the time!

Be Creative With Airports

You might want to think outside the box a little when it comes to airports. What I mean by that is there could be cheaper options than just the one airport that comes to your mind when thinking about your destination. If you're heading to Bermuda, maybe there really is only one airport and you don't have a choice. However, if you're heading to Europe, for example, the options are many. It is really easy (and usually cheap) to travel between cities and countries in Europe, either by train or by air. If you have several countries in mind that you want to visit, look into each country and find out what the best airport hubs are. For example, if you are going to Germany, you might find that Frankfurt is a better hub than Munich or Berlin, or right next door is Amsterdam, which is a huge European hub, or London, or... the list goes on. If you find a great deal into one airport but it's not where you wanted to go, check out www.easyjet.com and www.ryanair.com for cheap connecting flights within Europe. Just keep in mind that they often use different, smaller airports and have stricter baggage rules, but if you can save a lot of money it might be worth it.

You may also be able to save money by flying out of a different home airport. For example, Reno, NV was my closest home airport for a long time, but it tends to be much more expensive than San Francisco (SFO), which is three hours away. Maybe it isn't worth the stress for you to fly out of an airport that isn't the most convenient; on the other hand, maybe it is. I used to fly out of SFO all the time when I would go abroad. Sometimes it was even worth buying my international flight out of SFO or even LAX (Los Angeles) and getting a commuter flight down there on Southwest. If this does not sound like your cup of tea then be prepared to pay more if your airport is small.

For those of you planning a trip to Europe, you may want to consider this rather unique option that you won't soon forget: Icelandair offers flights from certain major US cities to major European cities with a stopover in Iceland at no extra charge. That's right, you could conceivably pay for one ticket and get two destinations out of it. Check it out at www.icelandair.us.

Plan For Changes You Don't Know You Might Need

There is one more factor to keep in mind when booking your flight: find out how easy or difficult it will be to change later if that becomes necessary. If you are as unpredictable as I can be, then it might be worth it for you to be able to change your flight at a later date. When I took my very first flight abroad to go study in Costa Rica when I was 18, I booked a flight with my study abroad program whose coordinator somehow knew that 85 college students would want 85 different return dates and would change their minds 85 times about said return dates. I'm glad the program staff knew what they were doing when they allowed us to buy tickets that were easy to change! It cost me a flat fee of $200 to push back my return date by one month, easy.

A few years later when I went on a three-month backpacking trip through Central America, I bought my first multi-city ticket. I flew into Panama City and was to

27

depart three months later out of Mexico City. Little did I know that I would fall in love with Guatemala and want to change my departure city so that I didn't even "have" to go into Mexico. I had booked a multiple airline ticket (the cheapest option at the time), and I was so excited to have found such a good deal that I didn't even consider the off-chance that I would need to change it later. When I did look into changing it, I found out that I would have had to change each ticket with each individual airline, which would include international and domestic ticket change fees, plus a difference of fare. Basically it would have probably been cheaper to buy a new one-way ticket home than to change the one I already had. I didn't see the value in that, so in the end I continued on to Mexico (which in hindsight I'm grateful for). I may have had a great week in Mexico, but the point is that I didn't prepare for the change I didn't know I wanted and therefore got stuck with what I had.

That being said, I certainly learned my lesson. A month later I booked a flight to South America, flying into Sao Paolo, Brazil, and departing three months later from Lima, Peru (how I love the multi-city flights!). This time, instead of booking with a general flight search engine, I booked directly through American Airlines, which meant all my flights were with American and would be easier to change if need be.

I started by conducting my original search through one of the websites on my flight search engine list and was lucky to find that American offered the complete itinerary at the lowest price I found (that doesn't always happen). At that point I went directly to www.aa.com (American Airline's website) to book. I found the exact same itinerary as I had on the other search engine, but instead of using a middleman, I was able to book directly. Pay attention to the airlines when you are searching with a flight search engine. If you are looking to buy a ticket in which all of the flights are provided by the same airline, ALWAYS go to the airline's website to book directly. You should be able to find that exact flight, and then your options are greater should you need to change your flight later.

"If you are looking to buy a ticket in which all of the flights are provided by the same airline, ALWAYS go to the airline's website to book directly."

This was the single best idea I had for this entire trip I was about to take, because in Brazil I ran into a rather big problem. This is a nightmare of a long story that I will save for another day but the outcome of it was that my only way out of my dilemma (and Brazil) was to change my flight completely. Standing at that American Airlines counter in the Sao Paolo airport with passport in hand and ticket fully issued through American Airlines was the easiest ticket change I have ever dealt with, and trust me, at that moment in my life, an easy way out was exactly what I needed. All I paid was the single international change fee of $200 plus the fare difference, which wasn't too bad and I was more than happy to pay for it at that moment. If I hadn't made the decision to book through American directly, I would have basically had to buy another ticket, the same situation I was in previously in Guatemala. Luckily when that happened to me in Guatemala I wasn't in dire straits like I was in Brazil. Keep this in mind if you think you might need to change your ticket! Or even if you don't think you'll need to, as traveling can be very unpredictable.

Once you find the right ticket and make it through the purchasing process (way to go!), keep a digital copy of it in your email and a paper copy in your backpack for the trip. It may come in handy at border crossings to prove onward transport.

Congratulations! You have completed the first (and sometimes the hardest) step towards making your trip a reality.

Chapter 3: Budgeting

I travel enough to make my friends wonder and ask me how I could possibly afford it. There are many ways to answer that question. For example, I don't have a car payment, I don't own a house, I chose an affordable college, earned scholarships and worked to put myself through school, so I don't have any student loans either. I think that's the kicker for most people. Yes, I pay for everything myself and always have. No I'm not a trust fund baby, not even close. I think it comes down to priorities, which I even wrote a challenging blog post about that is not to be missed. In my life, travel is a major priority, and I have my priorities straight. I work, and I save my money so I can travel. To me, it's just that simple. I have never been a big spender, and as that applies to all areas of my life, I am able to save more than the average person.

That's the nutshell about how I save when I'm in the States. I have also mastered the art of budget travel when I'm abroad. I have a number of tricks up my sleeve to accomplish this, and now I plan to share them with you.

It all starts with the plane ticket, a subject that I have already exhausted in Chapter 2. Getting the best possible deal on your plane ticket is the first major important step of budget travel, because every dollar you save on your ticket can be spent elsewhere on your travels. Let's get into some other areas of budgeting.

Budget Accommodations

After purchasing your plane ticket, the first thing you may want to look into is somewhere to stay. Some people like to plan out every day of their trip, which could be nice because then you don't have to think twice about all that planning, reserving, and booking later on. However, this type of planning ahead has its disadvantages too, because then you always have to be somewhere by a certain day or time (either that or you lose money on your reservation). It might make you wish you hadn't booked everything in advance so you could have a little more freedom with your time abroad. It's up to you. I have friends who never book anything in advance, but I prefer to book the first night or few so that I know exactly where I'm going the first day I arrive somewhere. I often leave it at that, and figure out my accommodations just a day or two ahead of time according to where I want to go.

If you are a "fly by the seat of your pants" sort of traveler, you may prefer not to make reservations. The reasons I do not prefer to travel like this are:

- I don't like the stress of not knowing where I'm going once I get somewhere, especially if it's a place I've never been before;

- Since I am a budget traveler, I like to know exactly what I will be paying or at least have a good idea of what it will cost;

- I want to feel like I got the best deal around and that the place where I'm staying will suit my needs.

When options are a click away on the computer, finding all of these things out ahead of time is very simple.

Alternatively, when your heavy backpack is weighing you down, you've been traveling all day, you're hungry (and grumpy), and you still have to walk all around town to find just the right place to stay, you might have wished you'd taken care of it previously. You might also not get a great deal because those who booked ahead took all the good rooms. I believe booking ahead saves time and money, two things I hate wasting. If I don't want to completely commit to one hostel or hotel, I will just book it for the first night in a new place, and then give myself a day to feel it out and perhaps change if I find something better in person. Win-win.

"I believe booking ahead saves time and money, two things I hate wasting."

For budget travelers and backpackers, I recommend staying at a hostel. There are thousands of them worldwide and they almost always prove to be interesting experiences. At hostels you pay by the bed, so you are literally only paying for yourself. This can be advantageous and save you money. It can also be a great way to meet other travelers. Many hostels also have the option of booking private rooms, so if you are in a small group, you may just find a hostel with the perfect number of beds in a private room. However, you still pay by the bed, and beds in private rooms are often a little bit more expensive. There are a handful of websites you can use to for search for hostels by country, city, and date, like the following:

- www.hostelworld.com

- www.hostels.com

- www.hostelsclub.com

- www.hostelbookers.com

Keep in mind, this information is up-to-date as of when this book was published and may have changed since then. It's always a good idea to do your own research, especially if it can help you save a buck. These websites will most likely offer the same hostels, and they will most likely be the exact same price. The trick about these websites is how they make their money.

The first three websites will charge you $2 per booking and require you to put 10% down. Now, $2 may not seem like much to you, however, if you are really on the go and will be moving around a lot, booking a lot of hostels, that $2 every time adds up very quickly. There are ways around paying the $2. On Hostels.com you can simply sign up for their email news and the $2 fee is waived. For Hostelworld.com you can either buy a gold card for $10 and then the fee is waived, or you can follow them on Twitter and every now and then they will put out codes for free gold cards that are valid for various lengths of time. On Hostelsclub.com you will also be charged a $2 booking fee, or you can purchase their membership card for 10 euros and it waives the fee. OR, you could simply go to the last one on the list, Hostelbookers.com and pay no booking fee. Pay attention to these tricks because if you are really interested in saving, every dollar matters! I like to start on Hostelworld because I like the user interface the best, and once I find the hostel I want, I book it on Hostels.com to save the $2 easily. It's all about taking advantage of the system, people.

"I like to start on Hostelworld because I like the user interface the best, and once I find the hostel I want, I book it on Hostels.com to save the $2 easily."

If you are traveling in a group, it may work out to be cheaper to book at a hotel where you pay by the room rather than the bed. Likewise, if you simply aren't interested in hostels, you may want to check out these websites:

- www.booking.com

- www.hotels.com

- www.asiarooms.com (Asia)

There is another site called www.airbnb.com that you may have heard of, and you can find some unique places that won't be listed elsewhere, but you also pay for it. Booking fees are figured by percentage of total sale and are much more expensive on this site. For hotels my favorite is Booking.com because I believe they have the best deals for a budget.

I recently went to Nicaragua with a group of friends and we had a brief planning meeting before we left to arrange accommodations. One of the girls had a specific place in mind where she wanted us all to stay and was looking directly on their website, telling us it would cost $120 per night. There were 6 of us, so this didn't sound so bad. However, I suggested we check the hostel websites anyway just to see what prices they offered. We ended up finding the exact same place, but it would only cost $90 per night. No catch. Obviously we ended up booking through the hostel website rather than directly through the merchant. We avoided the booking fee, too. For four nights, this saved us exactly $122, or just over $20 each. It literally pays to be budget-wise, so check all your options!

One time while my husband and I were in Bali, we picked out a hotel online and had a taxi take us there, however we had not yet booked a room. We thought maybe we could get a better deal by just walking in, so we decided to try it. We were wrong. Actually, the walk in price was literally about $90 *higher* than the price we had seen online for the exact same room. We weren't about to pay so much when we knew we could get a better deal. So, we politely excused ourselves for five minutes, used the free wireless and my iPhone to go onto Booking.com and reserve the room. Once the reservation went through, we went back up to the front desk and checked into our room at the price we had found online. Yes, we did. The staff at the front desk thought it was pretty funny, and they didn't mind at all that we were completely taking advantage of the system. In fact, they brought us welcome drinks and hot towels while we were waiting.

Couch Surfing

Some of you may have heard about one of latest crazes in travel: Couch Surfing. Yes, there is a real program called Couch Surfing (CS). My husband and I, and many people we know, participate one way or another in CS. It's not just something we do; it's something we are officially a part of. Now, I know what you might be thinking, "You people actually sleep on the couches of complete strangers!?" Yes, we do, and I can't really speak highly enough of this program. It is set up online sort of like Facebook. Your profile includes a bit about you, what you like, what interests you have, etc., as well as whether or not you are traveling or have a couch to offer. If you have a couch to offer, you tell a bit about your house, what your "couch" really is (whether it's a guest room or literally a couch- whatever the sleeping arrangements may be). You can have friends on CS and they can leave you references. What this means is that when someone views your profile, they will see who you are, what you are about, and what others have to say about you, either as a friend, a traveler, a guest, or a host. You can see the same information about others.

So how does it work? Start by setting up a profile and adding bits of information about yourself and your "couch" if you have one to offer. When you are traveling you can set your status to "Traveling" and that way no one will contact you to host them. Then when you need a couch to surf, you conduct a search by city. You can browse through the results and read about people who live in that city, and if you decide you'd like to stay with someone, you can submit a couch surfing request to them with dates and details. That person may then either accept or deny you for whatever reason. If someone accepts you, you work out arrival details via private messages and then go from there. That's it.

There is NO money exchange; Couch Surfing is about *cultural* exchange. Most of the people involved are genuinely interested in getting to know each other, which is why you include your interests in your profile. I have both surfed and hosted and have always liked the people I have met through this program. In fact, at our wedding last year we had three friends attend whom we had met on different occasions through CS. Three, at our *wedding*!

It is a safe program, and here's why: the power of references keeps it safe. Once you have surfed with or hosted someone, you are prompted and highly encouraged to write a reference for that person. You can give honest feedback with a positive, neutral, or negative reference. I have never seen a neutral or negative reference for anyone, that doesn't mean they don't exist. What better way to determine whether or not you want to stay with or host someone than by looking at his or her references? This is precisely how CS keeps its reputation as a safe program. Because of this feedback by other CSers, you can get an idea of what type of people you are dealing with, and you choose whom you would like to stay with, or whom you'd like to host.

There is more to Couch Surfing than just surfing couches. There are often social gatherings in each city. Believe it or not, there are usually people in each town who organize CS events. We attended one in Italy because we happened to be couch surfing with the CS organizer in the town we were visiting, and it turned out to be a really fun, international dinner party. The best part? We ended up couch surfing with a German couple we met there a couple months later when we were in

Germany. You never know who you're going to meet! You can get cultural insight through Couch Surfing in a way that you just can't get by staying at a hotel or even a hostel. And you'll meet new friends, *local* friends, along the way. It's a great way to travel on a budget as well since you don't pay for lodging. Just remember, thanking your hosts with a home cooked meal, a small gift, or even a drink will not go unnoticed! Check out CouchSurfing.org.

"It's a great way to travel on a budget as well since you don't pay for lodging."

Working And Volunteering Abroad

If you don't know where I'm headed with this and are wondering why I mention working abroad right along with budget accommodations, you may be in for a treat. If you have never heard of Workaway, Helpx, or Wwoofing (no, that's not a typo), allow me to introduce you. These three programs all have a major factor in common: they all offer work in exchange for room and board (to varying extents). These programs are magical. They allow travelers to live and work in one place, get to know locals, learn new skills or teach others some of their own, and collect rich life experiences through cultural work exchange, rather than money exchange.

These programs each have websites where you can browse through hosts worldwide. Hosts are people who have space to offer in exchange for your help with work that they need done. Each host has a profile, giving you as much information as you may need to make a decision about whether to go stay and work with them. Once you decide you would like to contact a host, you need to join the program. Yes, it costs money, but not very much, and yes it's worth it. At time of publishing, the amount you pay for Wwoofing depends on the country you want to host in; Workaway starts at 22 euros for a two-year registration; and Helpx is 20 euros for a two-year registration. Once you register, you can view the host's contact information, send private messages to them, and set up your stay.

The length of time you stay and work with a host varies by host. You can stay for one week or several months, depending on their rules, your preferences, or perhaps how things go. Usually working volunteers are expected to put in 4-5 hours per day of work in exchange for room and board, sometimes with a day or two off. All of these details vary greatly depending on the host. The type of work also varies. You can do anything from teaching a language, to cooking, to childcare, to gardening, to sustainable farming, to working in a hostel, to working on a yacht, to being an innkeeper and much more. The possibilities are literally endless. Beware, these websites are incredibly inspiring and you might find yourself daydreaming at work...

These three programs are great opportunities not only to save some money, but also to experience something local, with local people. I have used

Workaway once to get a job in Italy, and while we were there we had a co-worker who had found the job using Helpx. I know several people who have wwoofed all over the world and had very positive experiences. Here are the websites to get you started; happy volunteering!

- www.workaway.info

- www.helpx.net

- www.wwoof.net

If your goal in working abroad is to make money, you can try local websites like Craigslist, or try asking around. Very rarely do the hosts of the three programs previously mentioned ever offer to pay their workers. This would only occur if they need you to work the equivalent of a full-time job, and I have seen it happen only once. I had two jobs bartending the first time I lived in Italy. Both of them were cash jobs, and I got both of them simply by knowing the bartenders (and speaking Italian). I had another cash job years later in Rome that I found on Craigslist. Cash jobs are most likely what you will find without having to get a visa. It is possible to find jobs; you just have to look for them!

Budget Transportation

Public transportation is a great, economic way to travel, and it is pretty similar worldwide: trains, buses, subways, minibuses, collectives, shuttles, and even cheap flights. Since you are usually subject to the same prices as everyone else for public transportation, this section won't be very big, I just have a few specific points to cover.

A Note About German Trains

I used to think German trains were some of the most expensive in Europe. I once spent close to 90 Euros on a one-way ticket for a trip that should've taken about 3-4 hours. That's another story I will save for another day, but the point is that it was ridiculously expensive. Then one year a wise German friend of mine let me in on what I consider the best kept secret in Germany: regional train tickets. They are valid for up to five travelers, unlimited travel throughout any region of your choice (for one day), and they are cheap! One of these regional tickets will cost your entire group around 30-40 euros. They are called Länder Tickets; check them out at the train stations. The first time I tried it, I was traveling with 4 other people. We bought two Länder Tickets so we could freely pass between regions (Bavaria and Baden-Wuerttemberg to be exact), and we made it through every ticket check just fine, to my relief and disbelief. You can even purchase this type of ticket if you are traveling alone, so definitely take note if you will be traveling in Germany.

Cheap Flights Throughout Europe

As I mentioned in Chapter 2, Ryanair and easyJet airlines are fantastic and affordable options for getting across Europe. If you don't have any experience with them yet, you'll want to pay attention to this section. I once booked a flight from Frankfurt, Germany to Milan, Italy for 14 euros. I think it actually cost 99 cents, but with taxes it worked out to be 14 euros. You have a much better chance at getting a really great deal if you book as far in advance as possible. The most I've ever paid for a Ryanair or easyJet flight is 90 euros, which was over Christmas and rather last minute, from Frankfurt, Germany to Cádiz, Spain. The average flight is probably around 60 euros depending on timing and destinations. Check out www.ryanair.com and www.easyjet.com for cheap flights to all areas of Europe.

The major issues to be aware of when traveling with Ryanair and easyJet are the extra fees involved and the airports. It makes sense that if you are paying so little for a flight, there must be some sort of sacrifice. Those sacrifices come in the form of comfort and accessibility. The seats are rather small, do not expect a 747; this is a packed commuter flight. The baggage regulations are stricter than bigger commercial airlines and will always cost you money for checking luggage. Finally, the airports that Ryanair and easyJet use are not often the big, popular, convenient airports in most cities. In fact, you will often find that the airports they do use are outside of the city and will cost you a bit more in transportation fees to get to the city center. Be aware of this when you are booking. Most of the time it is still worth it and will still save you significant amounts money to fly with these two companies.

Here is another tip: much of Europe's public transportation functions on military time, or the 24-hour clock. Don't make the same mistake my brother once did by booking a cheap flight for 06:00 from England to Italy, only to find out that at 6pm (18:00), he wasn't going anywhere since he had missed his flight by about 12 hours.

"Much of Europe's public transportation functions on military time, or the 24-hour clock."

Student Discounts

If you have a student ID card, you may be eligible for discounts on travel abroad whether it is for flights or any other kind of public transportation. I'm not saying that your US College ID will be worth anything. However if you are studying abroad, be sure to get a student ID card through your program, because many places like to offer discounts for local students. You may also want to consider looking into getting a student ID card through www.statravel.com. I have never purchased this card, but some people say it's worth it. You must be a full time student to be eligible. If you are part of a study abroad program, be sure to find out from your program staff about all the discounts you are eligible for in your city or country. You may be able to get into museums and parks for discounted prices as well.

Budget Eating

Food is one of my favorite things, ever. One of my absolute favorite parts of traveling to foreign countries is trying their food, and I look forward to every meal and snack. Even if you don't love food as much as I do, I highly encourage you to experience a typical, local meal of your host country at least once, even if it means splurging a little bit. It is something to be experienced and a very important part of every country's culture.

Eating out for every meal is sometimes simply not in the budget though, so here are a few tips for staying on track with your budget and still getting to experience local food:

- Get creative at the grocery store, local markets, or with street vendors (don't be afraid of street food; use your best judgment);

- Get off the beaten path;

- Take advantage of a hostel kitchen.

First of all, I'm going to give you a couple examples of some of my favorite snacks in different countries. These are items that can be purchased at a grocery store and packed for lunch on a curb somewhere. In Italy I love to buy bread, cheese and some sort of salami (there are so many kinds!) and enjoy them together while people watching in a piazza somewhere. There is something very local about it, yet it doesn't cost me my entire food budget for the day. In Costa Rica, I like to buy tortilla chips at the store, an avocado, and a small can of refried beans with the easy-open cap. All you need to do is open the can of beans and the avocado and you have yourself some delicious dip options for your chips. It's a great snack for the beach, the bus, or wherever you may be. A local, freshly sliced mango might be the perfect addition to this meal. I recommend carrying some sort of camping knife/fork/spoon combination just for these types of situations.

One time when my husband and I were in South Korea, we were hungry but really had no idea where to go, until we saw a street vendor with a bit of a line. A line is almost always a good sign. We ended up waiting, for what we had no idea, but in the end we were served some hot fried dough with sugary, cinnamony, peanutty filling, a perfect snack for a freezing cold day. Another time in Thailand we happened upon a big open-air market. Since we hadn't had dinner yet, we indulged ourselves in all of the yummy food for sale. In the process we got to try several local foods that we hadn't seen yet in Thailand, and by the time we left with full bellies, we had spent only a few dollars.

Getting off the beaten path is great way to find quality, cheap food. Let me explain. I used to live in Rome, Italy, which is full of restaurants that I refer to as tourist traps. There are many chain restaurants that just don't do Italy the justice it deserves when it comes to cuisine. Unfortunately because of their convenient locations, they do quite well, and they can charge whatever they want (usually too much). The only reason I felt these were overpriced and not tasty enough is because I previously lived in Turin, Italy, up north in the Piemonte region, where the tourists were nearly non-existent, and the food was unbelievably delicious and cheap! I was determined to find real restaurants in Rome, and yes, I did find them. They are tucked way back up a street you'd never venture up, or enough out of the way that you simply wouldn't care to go that direction. We used to go to one place almost every week when we lived there, and I still daydream about my bowl of Penne al Salmone that I always ordered there. I very much look forward to eating there again next time I'm in Rome.

There is a popular town on the Caribbean coast of Costa Rica called Puerto Viejo, and my favorite place to eat lunch or dinner there is literally inside a chain-linked fence. No walls, just fence. Nearly one block down the street is a big tourist trap restaurant. I am willing to bet that the tourists who frequent that restaurant don't even order Costa Rican food there; they probably get some sort of comfort food because it is on the menu. On the other side of the street, within the chain linked fence is where you would find me, sipping my amazing jugo de piña drink with a typical Costa Rican casado in front of me, cooked fresh by the sweet women who work there. And there are only a few other tables at this restaurant, a true family-run place, where you know the food is going to be just plain good, not to mention cheap. If you aren't sure if you are walking into a tourist trap restaurant or not, just look around. If you see any locals, that's a good sign; if you see only tourists, you may want to think twice about what you really want to eat.

There are some places that are so expensive that it really is hard to stay within a budget. Hard, but not impossible. Take Paris for example, I found it to be one of the most expensive places I've ever been, not necessarily budget-friendly. My husband and I took advantage of street vendors selling amazing crepes for a price we could afford, and we frequented the grocery stores more than we wanted to. I mean, who doesn't want to go out and enjoy French food while in Paris? But it was hard with our budget. We cooked meals in the kitchen where we were staying, but we made sure to have a real French dinner with one of my Parisian friends one of the nights that we were there. I don't feel like we missed out, and we were able to be smart about our money.

I realize there are credit cards for this, but as a person who doesn't stress over debt (because I don't have any), I urge you to stay within your means. This is the purpose of having a budget.

I mentioned having used the kitchen where we were staying in Paris, and this can be a real money-saver. It doesn't mean you can't try local food. Get something new and different at the grocery store, along with a cheap bottle of wine, and cook it yourself in your hostel with your new hostel buddies. I almost always get a hostel with a kitchen when I have the option. It is possibly the most budget-friendly thing about hostels, and you won't be alone. Making friends in the kitchen at hostels is almost inevitable and a great part of the experience of budget traveling. This is why I don't feel like I miss out when I just can't afford to eat out every night.

Being smart about your money will take you far when you are abroad. The last thing a traveler wants is to run out of money, or end up with a huge credit card bill. The smarter you are with budgeting from the very beginning, the longer your current trip can be, and the sooner your next trip can be. Make decisions about budgeting before you go. This is a good idea for two reasons: one, because when you are in the moment, it is easy to give in to an expensive dinner or that extra activity that you don't really need to pay for; and two, you may not be on the same budget as some of your fellow travelers. If your decisions about budget are made before your trip, it is easier to stick to them.

"The smarter you are with budgeting from the very beginning, the longer your current trip can be, and the sooner your next trip can be."

Chapter 4: Packing: Less Is More

Try not to be intimidated, packing is fun! It is the final step in anticipation and preparation for your trip. The best part is that when you're done, you will actually be ready to go! The hardest part of packing is deciding what to bring, and for some that includes knowing how to bring it. Do you know if it's better to bring a backpack or a suitcase? Do you know where and how to find a good backpack? Do you know what to put in it?

What Does Your Luggage Look Like?

Let's start with your packing vessel(s). If you don't plan to be moving around a lot or climbing onto a lot of buses or trains, you may consider bringing a suitcase. If you're going on a leisurely vacation or even a business trip, bring a suitcase if you want. Alternatively, if you're going to be moving around a lot on an adventurous trek, bring a backpack. Finally, if you're studying abroad for up to a year, I have found that a medium suitcase *and* a backpack for your shorter trips are just about perfect. If you only need to bring one piece of luggage to study abroad, I would recommend a backpack over a suitcase for convenience on the shorter trips you are bound to take.

As for carry-ons, a big purse, shoulder bag or messenger bag of some sort should suffice. Make sure it's something very comfortable that you can carry for days (because you will be doing just that). If you're bringing a backpack, keep in mind that your carry-on should fit well and be somewhat easy to handle along with your backpack, because you will have to carry both whenever you're transitioning. The lighter and smaller your luggage, the better your attitude will be. A small backpack you can wear across your front is good for this, or an over-the-shoulder purse or bag is also fairly easy to manage. Here's another tip: make sure it has a functioning zipper. There is an article on my website devoted to exactly what I pack *in* on a backpacking trip.

Three Things To Look For In A Good Backpack

If you don't have a good backpack and you plan on doing a lot of moving around, I suggest you buy one. It is very important that you find a good backpack that fits you. There are three specific things you should look for when you go searching for a good backpack, the three C's: comfort, convenience, and capacity. Comfort is ultra important as you will be wearing this backpack for days on end sometimes, and nobody likes a sore and grumpy travel buddy. Convenience has to do with how easy it is to pack, unpack, access things at the bottom, and stuff items conveniently where you need them (like easy-access top or outside pockets). Capacity of course is how much it will hold, and this is a really important factor when deciding on a backpack. Don't decide on capacity simply by the length of time you will be traveling; rather, let your body size and strength be your deciding factor.

"Don't decide on capacity simply by the length of time you will be traveling; rather, let your body size and strength be your deciding factor."

The first backpack I traveled with was not only a size too big for me, it was entirely too large for what I needed, which led to over packing and very sore shoulders, not to mention a bad attitude. This is why it is important to get measured for the right size. When you go in to get fit for a backpack, ask them to fill it up for you (if they don't have the means to do this, you might as well leave and go to the next store). Test it full and heavy, because it will be full and heavy when you actually use it. You should be able to tell right away what you can handle. If you can't tell, maybe my story will help. My first backpack was a medium 65 + 10, which means medium torso with a carrying capacity of 65 liters that can be expanded to 75 liters. My current backpack is a Gregory Jade 50, size small. That's a huge and critical difference! It fits me well and is still comfortable when it's packed full. This comfort should be your deciding factor for determining capacity. Then you just need to get creative with packing light to work with the capacity that you have, which is the weight and comfort that you know you can handle.

Where Do You Get A Good Backpack?

I have done a bit of searching for backpacks, and the best service I have experienced is at REI. If you are lucky enough to have an REI near you, I highly recommend paying a visit and asking their experts to fit you for a backpack. As in, don't bother looking anywhere else; you will find all your answers at REI.

If you don't have an REI near you, you can still check out their website (www.rei.com) for expert advice about choosing the right backpack (size charts, etc.), or you can always make a visit to your local recreational sports store. If it is your first time buying a backpack, it really would do you well to get fitted by staff that knows what they are doing. Just remember, don't automatically believe anyone when they say you need a 65+ backpack (or anything entirely too big) simply because you will be gone for a long time. I am 5'7" and weigh 125 pounds. Remember that giant backpack I used to have? I eventually sold it to a male friend of mine who is probably 6' tall and 200 pounds. It fits him. I learned my lesson, and I'd like for you to learn it too, the easy way.

Once you have been fitted and/or figure out which backpack size you want to get, buy it. If you want a budgeting secret, then I recommend ordering your backpack from the REI Outlet at www.rei.com/outlet. This is where they sell their clearance and marked down items, and I can almost guarantee that you will find a good deal on the right backpack for you, not to mention you'll save a few bucks! You can also find many backpacks marked down on Amazon. Just keep one thing in mind: when it comes to a backpack, don't sacrifice comfort for money. It will be worth the few extra bucks to get just the right backpack for you.

"I recommend ordering your backpack from the REI Outlet at www.rei.com/outlet."

Three Things To Look For In A Good Suitcase

There are a few things to keep in mind when looking for a good suitcase: size (not just the obvious capacity, I'll explain), structure, and quality. Have you ever seen those oversized suitcases? Yeah, don't go there, they encourage overpacking and are anything but convenient on the road. Somewhere in between those oversized suitcases and carry-ons is ideally what you should look for.

More space is not always a good thing because not only does it encourage overpacking, but it also becomes extremely heavy in the process. Also keep in mind that if you will be towing it behind you down narrow aisles, whether it be on planes, trains, or buses, you will want a narrow suitcase. Sometimes narrow and deep is better than shallow and wide. Don't be that person who hits everyone's elbows and causes traffic jams down the aisle; plan ahead. Take a look at the structure and organization of the suitcase and make sure it has all the compartments, wheels, and pulleys that you might need. Lastly, keep in mind that no airline employee cares about your bag. Period. This is where quality comes in. The stronger and better the quality of the suitcase, the less likely that it will rip or break in transport.

When purchasing a new suitcase, always check out the latest deals on Amazon, and don't count out stores like Ross and TJ Maxx where you can save on brand names. One more tip: if you must buy a wide suitcase, try finding one with four wheels (rather than two) on the bottom so you can roll it sideways down those aisles.

"When purchasing a new suitcase, always check out the latest deals on Amazon, and don't count out stores like Ross and TJ Maxx where you can save on brand names."

What To Put In Your Luggage

Once you have carefully selected your packing vessels, you are probably going to stare at them blankly wondering how the heck to fill them. Packing light is definitely a creative art. It means leaving behind that pair of shoes you might need if you come across a certain occasion, or the extra three shirts when you already have five, or six bathing suits when you really only need one or two... you get the picture. If you have any kind of a budget for buying souvenirs, or in my case clothing and accessories abroad, you will be glad you packed light and saved yourself the extra space and weight. There are some tricks to creating space while packing, but let's get to that in a bit.

I always start with a nicely made bed. Across the bed is where I spread everything I'm thinking about packing so I can see it all laid out before me. The first things I collect for packing are all the gadgets (non-clothing items) I will need. Some ideas for these items include:

- **Cameras, memory cards, mini tripods (whatever your accessories are), and battery chargers;**

- **iPod, headphones, and charger:** if you have a newer iPod or iPhone, here's a cool tip- your charger (that little white box that plugs into the wall and has the USB input for your phone) is actually a converter, which means you shouldn't need to worry about voltage;

- **Outlet adapter:** generally these are just adapters, not converters, so be aware of voltage (more about converters and voltage in Chapter 8);

- **Toiletries:** remember not to pack any liquids over 4 oz. or sharp items that will be taken from you in your carry-on;

- **Pills:** think ahead, you may want pain killers, fiber pills, anti-diarrhea pills, motion sickness pills, try to bring what you might need, these are much cheaper and easier to find Stateside, especially if you are heading into a language barrier;

- **Sunscreen:** it is surprisingly expensive in many foreign countries;

- **Small dry bag** if necessary;

- **PASSPORT and immunization card:** I keep these together so as to not forget the card;

- **Travel towel** if necessary;

- **Sarongs:** these wonderful inventions have multiple purposes. Not only do they pack nice and small (I don't bother with bulky towels anymore), but you can also take them to the beach or use them for sheets or pillowcases or even a skirt or dress, and their light material dries quickly most of the time. If you don't have one yet and you're headed to the beach, don't worry; odds are you'll have plenty of options to buy one once you get there.

- **Headlamp:** you never know when you might need a flashlight, and they pack small;

- **Shoes:** flip-flops, comfortable walking shoes, versatile sandals or boots that can be dressed up (girls), and any other activity-specific shoes you may need. Check out the packing category on my blog for more help with shoes;

- **Journal;**

- **Kindle or book;**

- **Sleeping essentials:** earplugs, sleeping pills if you think you'll need them (I can't leave home without my Benadryl), eye mask;

- **Watch:** for those times that you don't have a cell phone and need to know what time it is, and you may also occasionally need to be able to set an alarm;

- **Travel wallet:** I actually have a specific wallet I use when I travel; it fits in my pocket and only carries cash and a card or two;

- **Safety pins:** a must;

- **Small combo lock(s):** for hostel lockers;

- **One or two plastic bags;**

- **Chapstick:** I can't leave home without it;

- **Itinerary:** Make sure you have a paper copy of your flight or trip itinerary.

These are examples of non-clothing essentials that I usually take with me. Some of those items may seem strange to you, but they do serve a purpose. Let me elaborate on a few: the combo locks, safety pins, flip-flops and plastic bags. Make sure your combo lock is small, not your typical high school locker-sized lock, but rather a small one that is not only lighter and takes up less space, but that also has a smaller bar that will fit into many more shapes and sizes of holes for locks. I have been known to bring two; it doesn't hurt to be prepared. As for safety pins, bring a small handful; they are great for holding zippers shut, repairing clothes, backpacks, even sunglasses when the screws fall out. Yes, I have done that. You would be amazed at the many uses for safety pins. As for the flip-flops, let's just say communal hostel showers are not always clean places, and you don't want to end up with some strange foot fungus now do you? Flip-flops pack small; even if you don't plan to wear them out, bring them for the showers. Lastly, plastic bags are great for dirty laundry, wet or muddy clothes, or even water-proofing if you need it, plus they pack small.

Next, I decide which clothes I will need. Here is the creative part: if you bring fewer items that can mix and match more, you make better use of your limited space. Less is more. Even if you are going for a month or more, you should only need as much clothing as if your trip were for just two weeks. Pack for two weeks, and learn to stretch it once you get abroad. Go for the clothing items that have the most versatility, from jeans that can be long or rolled up into capris, to flip flops that can be casual or dressy, to shirts that can be layered for warmth. Also keep in mind, especially if you like to shop, you will most likely be purchasing a few new items of clothing abroad.

"Even if you are going for a month or more... pack for two weeks, and learn to stretch it once you get abroad."

If you aren't sure about what the weather will be like where you're headed, look it up and look at weather trends from past years. If it tends to be rainy, bring a small, light umbrella or packable raincoat. If it will be cold, try to bring your most versatile jacket, and remember that layering your clothes is a great tool for keeping warm. Most hostels offer some kind of laundry service so you can plan on washing and re-wearing your clothes as often as you need. If you want to be extra prepared, buy a travel pack of laundry detergent so you can wash your clothes in the sink if you don't have laundry service available. One thing I make sure to do is bring lots of underwear, because if it turns out you can't find laundry service for a while, at least you have plenty of clean underwear; the rest of your clothes can wait.

Packing It All Up

Once I have all of these items collected before me, I separate them into what I will carry on with me and what I will check (if I am checking a bag at all). As for the gadgets, I generally carry my electronic devices on the plane with me because they are most valuable to me. That way, I know the airline can't possibly lose them. I also put my wallet, passport, itinerary, chapstick, kindle/book, and even some toiletries (deodorant, toothbrush and paste, makeup bag) in my carry-on. The rest will go into my checked luggage. For my clothes, I bring just one change of clothes with me in my carry-on, and the rest go into my checked luggage. I have been the victim of misplaced luggage enough to learn to pack that one change of clothing in my carry-on, just in case.

Once you think you have collected everything you need for your carry-on and checked luggage, pack your bags accordingly. Pack them completely just to make sure everything fits, and if you need to take some items out, this is when you'll find out and have to make the cuts.

There are a few tricks that people use to save space in luggage. For example, you could roll your clothes or stuff them in Ziploc bags, extracting all possible extra air. I've never gotten into either of these habits, but to each their own. One space-saving trick I have learned is that if you are going to buy any toiletries or really anything that comes in a box, pack the whole box. You can open it up and throw the boxes away when you get abroad, and presto, more souvenir space. If you end up bringing several different types of pills, you could put them all in one small bottle, and label the outside accordingly so you don't forget what is what.

You may want to look into baggage restrictions for your specific airline before you go. Many airlines will charge extra (a *lot* extra) for bags weighing over a certain amount, and you don't want that to be your bag! In most cases it's a completely unnecessary expense.

Avoid Checking Bags If Possible

One way to avoid baggage inconveniences altogether is to not check any bags. That's right, pack light, take small enough luggage that you can carry it on the plane with you (my Gregory Jade 50 is small enough to carry-on!), and you'll see the advantages are many:

- You won't be charged for a checked bag, eliminating baggage fees on every flight;

- You won't need to spend extra time waiting for your bag to show up at the baggage claim; and,

- My favorite: you will never have to worry about the airline losing or damaging your luggage!

All you need to do is make sure you don't have any items packed that won't make it through airport security. If I am really going to need one or two things that I know won't make it through security, whether they are sharp gadgets or oversized liquids, I make a plan to purchase these items once I am abroad. Simply brilliant? You're welcome. Problem solved, and I will probably spend way less on these couple of items than I would have on checked luggage.

I have recently started packing just carry-on luggage whenever possible. I say whenever possible because various situations require various types of packing, and sometimes it just doesn't cut it to bring only a carry-on. However, it is so much more rewarding than I ever realized, and after having had my share of lost or delayed luggage, I will continue to carry on whenever I can. My backpack is within the limits of carry-on luggage size, so I try not to pack it full and it works just fine. I also have a smaller backpack, a 30 (compared to my 50), for short trips, and traveling with that one is fabulously easy.

Packing from start to finish may take you a few hours or more, but it doesn't need to take you days. Some people start "packing" weeks in advance, and I have never understood this. If you have a checklist of items you need to buy like adaptors, extra batteries, sunscreen, travel laundry detergent, etc., then be aware of that list and make sure you have everything you need before you start packing, but you don't need to start packing it up too early! It will assuredly result in the tearing apart of your suitcase or backpack the day before you leave just to make sure you packed everything anyway.

Once you have gathered everything you think you'll need and you've determined that everything fits and have made final decisions about what to bring, pack it all up hours before you leave, and zip it or clip it shut. Make sure your necessary documents and passport are in hand and hope you didn't forget anything. Congratulations, you are ready to get on a plane!

Chapter 5: Leaving It All Behind

I suppose there are some logistics behind my "Just go!" attitude. You can't really just up and leave without taking care of some things Stateside first. Perhaps I should put it this way, you could just up and leave, but you might find yourself in some trouble later if you don't pay mind to a few things first. If you plan to be abroad for a long period of time, either traveling, working, or studying abroad, here is a list of some questions you should consider before you go:

- What do you do about your US cell phone account?

- Should you move out, rent your room, put your stuff in storage?

- What bills do you need to cancel, freeze, or make sure are on autopay?

- Who is going to handle your finances if something important comes up?

What To Do With Your US Cell Phone Account

I'll address the cell phone account first. Most cellular phone companies will allow you to freeze your account for a certain period of time, which is a great tool for saving money if you plan to be gone for a while. Make a call to your cellular carrier customer service and look into your options. This is the best way to save money on your cell phone bill while you aren't using it. This is regarding your US account alone, not your actual phone. Check out Chapter 8 for more fun facts about what you can do with your smartphone abroad.

You might have a cellular carrier that has the ability to make and receive calls overseas, but this does *not* mean you should take advantage of that. You might not like the sight of your phone bill after you've been making and receiving calls from abroad. Therefore, unless you do have some sort of international plan, I would advise against using your phone for calls or any data usage (not on Wi-Fi) if your US account is still active while you're abroad. However, if you can connect your phone to Wi-Fi, you should be able to access the same things abroad that you would in the States via Wi-Fi, and it shouldn't cost you anything.

When I go abroad with my US account still active (for shorter trips), I switch my phone to airplane mode just to be sure I won't accidentally use any data. I do, however, love being able to access the Internet, apps (especially Voxer), and even iMessages over Wi-Fi with my iPhone. The only restriction is that it has to be connected to Wi-Fi for that all to work.

That all being said, you may also have the option to unlock your smartphone and use it abroad through a *foreign* carrier, which I will explain in Chapter 8. However, you can still achieve this *and* freeze your account at home so you aren't wasting money Stateside while you're gone.

What To Do With Your Stuff

If you will be out of the country for several months at a time, you are probably planning to move out of wherever you live, so as to not pay rent, or perhaps you will at least sub-lease your room for the time you are away. I have never sublet a room, I just move out and move on. Either way, you may need to find a place to put all your stuff.

This is where it pays to not be a pack rat. Through my years of most frequent traveling, I owned no furniture that wasn't collapsible or plastic, and if I did acquire something for a temporary period of time (like a bed), then I would sell it before I took off again. Everything I owned used to fit in the back of my Toyota truck, proving to be very convenient for how much I moved, which quite often was into a storage unit.

When it comes to a storage unit, in the interest of being on a budget, do a bit of shopping around so you can find a good deal. I once hauled my stuff almost an hour away to a storage unit because it was literally half the price of the storage units where I lived. It had the same level of security, same basic storage unit, but was just in a different town. That was absolutely worth it to me to save that much money for every month that I was gone. Paying for a storage unit is much better than paying for rent, and if you are worried about any of your stuff you can always get extra insurance on it. Also, make sure you aren't paying too much for a storage unit. Get rid of your cheap furniture if you can. Let me elaborate. If you own a $70 bed and a $50 couch, yet you store it and end up paying an extra $50 per month for that larger storage unit, who is losing money? Yes, you. Sell what you can and just store the important things you can't part with. Pack it up, say a temporary goodbye, and get ready for your adventure.

Staying On Top Of Your Bills

The least you can do to get your bills organized is go through all of them and make sure they are all on autopay if you have the option to make it that way. You don't want to be late on your bills and in turn have late fees as you are traveling abroad. If you have the option to freeze any bills that won't be applicable while you are abroad, definitely look into that. For example, your car insurance does not need to be paid while your car is sitting (as long as no one is driving it). Perhaps your health insurance can be frozen, unless it covers you abroad. I will get into travel insurance more in Chapter 8. If you have renter's insurance you can probably freeze or even cancel it if you move out of your place.

Simply be aware of all of your bills. There are some things you do not want to worry about or waste precious money on while you are abroad. Make sure there is enough money in the assigned autopay account and that they are set up to take care of themselves. If possible, freeze or even cancel some to lessen your monthly payments. It is likely that you will be able to monitor your bills online if you need to, but you never know when you won't be able to access the Internet abroad, and you don't want to miss any deadlines.

"Be aware of all of your bills... make sure they are set up to take care of themselves."

Financial Matters At Home

I would recommend selecting a highly trusted friend or family member to take care of anything legal or financial that may come up and need personal attention while you are away. I would also recommend entrusting someone as your mail monitor to go through your mail and notify you if anything needs immediate attention. This way, if an important letter comes for you in the mail you know that someone will find it, or if a check comes you know someone will deposit it.

Up until just a couple of years ago, my parents' address was my permanent mailing address since I moved around so much. I could count on them to identify important mail and let me know if something needed to be taken care of, and usually they could even take care of it for me. Appoint someone you trust to be your mail monitor so you can rest assured you aren't missing anything important.

One time my mother and I signed a Power of Attorney agreement which gave her the right to make legal decisions for me in my absence, and I also gave her access to my bank accounts just in case anything came up. I don't think a Power of Attorney is necessary for everyone, but I had just turned 18 at the time and was about to leave for the first time for a year, so I had no idea what to expect. If your situation could use a Power of Attorney, perhaps you should look into it.

The reason for taking care of all these things is simple: your stuff is your responsibility. If you have the option to save yourself both money and stress, wouldn't you choose to do so? By organizing what you will be leaving behind in the States, you will be making your life abroad that much more enjoyable and stress-free.

Chapter 6: Being Safety-Smart

There is a saying, "Learn from other people's mistakes; life is too short to make them all yourself." Let this chapter be many safety lessons in learning from other people's mistakes! Don't let this section scare you or deter you from traveling, rather, let it prepare you to be a safety-smart traveler.

Not many avid travelers can say they have never lost anything or had something stolen during their travels to all ends of the earth. I once had my emergency money (a $100 bill) stolen right out of the money belt that I left safely locked in my hotel room. Yes, that means that one of the cleaning ladies rooted through my stuff, found the bill and made off with it. Luckily she left my passport, which was in the same pocket, but it still hurt to lose $100 as I was trying to pinch pennies traveling through Central America. I thought my belongings were safe in my locked hotel room, and I was wrong. I had it stuffed deep in an inside pocket of my backpack and she still found it. You can never be too sure. One of the most important items you can bring with you while traveling is a lock of some sort. Many hostels and hotels offer lockers but don't provide locks. Locking up your valuables is up to you.

I find it somewhat ironic that the hotel where my $100 was stolen was actually the nicest hotel I stayed in throughout my entire three-month Central America trip. It was in Guatemala and I was with a friend who had had enough of hostels at that point and splurged to let us stay at a beach resort for a couple of days. Lesson learned here is don't trust it just because it looks nice! Your valuable belongings are valuable to others as well.

I find that hostels are generally really safe places. I say generally because there are exceptions to everything. However, for the most part everyone at a hostel is there for the same reason and has the same reservations about their things being stolen; thus creating somewhat of a level of trust between roommates. Many backpackers choose to leave their valuables out on their beds in plain view. I would not recommend this. There must be a reason why in the last 10 years the only thing I have lost while traveling is that $100 that was stolen from me, so I'm going to share and elaborate on some common sense tips for you.

- Bring a lock or two; make sure you know the combinations! Don't bring key-locks; you could lose those small keys.

- Keep your bags in your sight on public transportation.

- Ladies (and guys with man-bags) bring purses that ZIP closed.

- Keep a mental note of where all of your valuables are all the time (iPod, passport, cash, credit cards, camera, etc).

- Learn to recognize distraction traps that, if you get caught in, will lead to the theft of your valuables!

Keep Your Luggage In Sight

The single most important tip is to use your common sense! Be in control of your belongings and aware of your surroundings. If you find yourself on public transportation of some kind, keep your purse/daypack/man-bag in your lap or at your feet with one strap looped through your leg (so someone can't reach under the seat in front or behind you and pull it away literally right under your nose). If there are racks above your head for bags, put your bag *across* the aisle and in front of your seat so that you can always keep an eye on it. I have friends from my study abroad programs who put their bags directly above their heads and guess what? You can't see it, nor can you see if someone decides to take it when they get off the bus, and then it's too late. There go their cameras and all of their memories! If you put it across the aisle then you have a clear view of it every time someone goes to retrieve a bag, and with your eye on it, it's not going anywhere fast.

*"If there are racks above your head for bags, put your bag **across** the aisle and in front of your seat so that you can always keep an eye on it."*

If there are compartments underneath the bus and you have no choice but to put your backpack there, then do everything you can to get a seat on that side of the bus so you can watch every time the bus pulls over to let someone off and they open the compartment doors. Don't sit so the doors will block your window when they are lifted open; sit behind or in front of them so you have a clear view of the luggage being unloaded. Bags can and will be stolen this way, so pay attention to yours! If you fall asleep you are taking the risk that your bag might be stolen while you're sleeping, so either secure it to yourself before you nod off or hope that it will still be there when you wake up.

I know I only mentioned public transport above, but this goes for rental cars as well. It is safer for you to bring your belongings inside your hotel than to leave them locked in a car full of windows. Please don't leave your passport and money in your car. If you do, you are just asking for it. I met a guy at the Houston airport on the way back from Costa Rica in 2010 who had nothing but his daypack for luggage. As it turned out, his entire suitcase had been stolen out of his rental car that was broken into while it was parked in a small beach town in

Costa Rica. A small beach town that I know quite well and happen to think is a safe area, so again, don't trust it just because it looks safe. Fortunately he had his passport and wallet with him in his daypack.

The Trick About Zippers And Safety Pins

Speaking of daypacks, purses, and man-bags, a zip-close bag can be essential for keeping your valuables safe. I've always carried a purse that zips and here's a secret: carry safety pins as well! One tricky use for safety pins is pinning your zipper shut, that way you can wear the bag behind your back without worrying if someone is slowly opening your zipper. One tug on that safety pin and you are bound to feel it before the thief even realizes what's stopping him or her.

It is not uncommon to see travelers wear their daypacks in front rather than on their backs for extra security. If this will make you feel better, do it. The safety pin zipper trick is great for that nap you wanted to take on the train while your purse is in your lap, too. Sometimes I will leave all my zippers pinned while I'm in transit so I don't have to worry about pockets opening. Putting key rings through double zippers that pull in opposite directions is a good idea as well. Your goal should be to make the thief give up on you. Your job is to look after yourself; respectively, everyone else needs to take care of themselves, so share your tricks with your travel buddies!

This brings to mind an unfortunate but very good example. I was once on the metro in Rome with a German friend who wore an over-the-shoulder strap purse that used to clip closed but the clip on the cover flap was broken. I hope you can already see what's wrong with this picture. We stood in the middle of the crowded (shoulder to shoulder) metro car and she took her hand off of her purse. When we got off and walked out of the building, she stopped to buy a soda only to realize that her wallet was missing out of her purse. Amidst an outburst of cussing and yelling (in German, no less) and not being able to blame it on anyone but herself, we figured someone stole it in the moment she took her hand off her purse.

It was an unfortunate turn of events, but perhaps if she had been wearing a purse that zipped closed, or at least one that did not have a broken clip, she might still have that wallet today. We spent that entire day dealing with her embassy, as we were going back to Germany the next day and she had no ID. Not my idea of a Roman holiday. Get a purse that zips closed, hold it under your arm, safety-pin it closed, do whatever it takes; don't make it easy for someone to steal from you!

"Get a purse that zips closed, hold it under your arm, safety-pin it closed, do whatever it takes; don't make it easy for someone to steal from you!"

If you do find yourself without your passport, if either you lost it or it was stolen, you are going to need to get a new temporary one issued from your embassy. Locate your nearest embassy and ask them for help. It will greatly benefit you if you happen to still have some form of identification with you. This may be a good reason to bring your driver's license or a school ID (photo ID is best) if you have one and just pack it away in your bag somewhere for a backup plan. You may want to think ahead and get passport photos taken before you go to the embassy as well, just to speed up the process. Better yet, don't let any of it happen in the first place.

Keep Inventory Of Your Valuables

I find myself doing mental checks of my valuables every now and then when I'm abroad, just to remind myself of where all my important items are. I usually have my cash, camera, and iPod on me; sometimes I even carry my passport if I think I'll need it. I have a money belt that I don't wear (no need to laugh), but I use it to store my back-up credit card, emergency cash, passport, immunization record, and copy of my flight itinerary, and I leave it locked up in my hostel, unless for some reason I doubt the security of the room. I often think that my most valuable items are the safest when they are with me, and I believe this because I have never been robbed.

On the other hand, I have some friends from a study abroad program who weren't so lucky. Kari and Andy were walking together at night in Costa Rica and were robbed by a couple of guys with knives. There was even a girl with these guys who stood by and did nothing. My friend Kari had to give up her entire purse, they wouldn't even let her keep her lip-gloss. Our friend Andy, who happened to be going home to the US the very next day, had to give them his camera and iPod, but at least the two were not hurt in the process. Robberies like this are not commonplace, but they can certainly happen to anyone, anywhere.

The best way to avoid them is by completely avoiding the situation (dark alleys, walking alone at night, etc.). When I have the option, if I am walking down an empty street at night, I will walk right down the middle of the road. This would give me just an extra bit of time to react to someone coming out of nowhere. If I have a set of keys with me, I will carry them in my fist so the keys stick up between my fingers. It's just one more line of defense in case something should happen, who knows if it would actually work, but these are just things I have learned to do.

In the end, carrying valuables with you is risky, but these are the risks of traveling that you just have to be aware of and try to be smart about. Did Andy need to be carrying his iPod and camera that night? Did Kari really need her whole purse for wherever she was going? Perhaps they really did and were just unlucky, or perhaps they could have avoided some of it by either taking a taxi or leaving some items at home.

I'm a fan of carrying money and my point and shoot camera in my pockets if I can; it's also more comfortable for me than wearing a purse all day. One time I actually transferred the contents of my purse into my pockets because I felt I was walking in an area that had the potential to be dangerous. My thought that night was that if someone goes for my purse, they can have it, and maybe I'd have a chance to run away with my valuables in my pockets. Once again, you never know what will work or won't work until you are in the situation, and hopefully it won't ever come to that. The only thing you can do is try your best to be aware and be prepared.

Speaking of keeping money in pockets, I have a well-traveled friend who always keeps about $20 worth of whatever currency he's using in his pockets. He has done a lot of traveling in the Third World, and he has found this to be helpful in warding off robberies. If he has some money right there in his pocket, he can offer it up to the person demanding of him, whether it's corrupt authorities or individuals demanding money for passage or even someone who wants to rob your person. Apparently if you have money to offer right away, sometimes they will take it and run, or let you by without doing a search. In the end, it's just a bit of money. Thankfully I have never been in a situation like this, but I do see the value in his idea.

When I was traveling in Brazil by myself en route to Bolivia, I wore an elastic money band on my calf under my jeans. In it I put my credit cards, money, passport, and my camera's memory cards. I had heard too many horror stories about buses getting pulled over and robbed during the night in Brazil. I didn't want to take any chances with my most important items. As it turned out, I ran into that huge problem I mentioned in Chapter 2 and ended up in San Francisco, not Bolivia, all the while still wearing my money band. Sometimes it helps to find humor in bad situations. At least I knew if anything happened I would still have my essentials, even my photos. This type of money band is actually meant for a man's arm, but fits perfectly under jeans or skirts. I would highly recommend something like this for anyone who wants to be prepared or needs to put their mind at ease.

Don't Fall Victim To The Tourist Trap

Not all robberies happen right in front of your face; some actually happen right behind your back. There is a trick that many thieves have learned: they work in pairs or even groups. While one does something to distract you, the other is slowly pulling open your zipper (which isn't fastened with a safety pin) behind your back, or making off with your bag that you momentarily deserted to "help" the distracter. Don't fall victim to this trick! Remember that one of your highest priorities is keeping, not just keeping track of, but actually keeping your valuables. Some friends of mine were once traveling in Italy on a train when a man near them dropped all of his coins. In the time it took them both to bend over and help the man pick it all up, someone (most likely his partner in crime) had stolen their iPods and laptop right from their seats. Awesome.

"Not all robberies happen right in front of your face; some actually happen right behind your back."

One afternoon, my good friend Ban was walking along a crowded sidewalk in Turin, Italy. She took notice of a guy near her acting very awkwardly and then he suddenly made eye contact with her and glanced behind her. She later assumed his glances were accidents (probably an amateur), because she quickly clued in and whipped around to find another guy trying to unzip her backpack. Fortunately, both of the guys took off running after they'd been caught in the act, but if she hadn't figured it out, she would have most likely lost her wallet which was right there in the pocket he was unzipping.

This is precisely the type of situation where it would be beneficial to safety pin your zippers shut or wear your backpack in front of you. Luckily she was walking (not standing still) and actually wearing her backpack, because in just the few seconds it took for her to realize what was happening, the two guys could have easily made off with the bag had it been unattended by her feet.

If you have seen the movie *Oceans 12* you might remember a scene near the beginning where Matt Damon is involved in an unbelievable exchange of pick pocketing. Well, believe it, because these guys are real, they get lots of practice, and they are good. Guys who wear loose jeans should be especially concerned, because they are less likely to feel anything. Man-bags are cool, and they are a smart alternative to loose pockets. Be a man and embrace them, they could save you a lot of trouble someday. Or, you can try switching your wallet to your front pocket, which would also greatly hinder the process if not prevent it altogether.

The key to being prepared for an incident like this is being able to recognize what's going on. For example, if someone drops something, or asks you to take their photo (yes, even a nice looking couple), or stops you to ask directions, or asks you for some sort of favor, or just seems to be acting strangely, look around first before you jump in to help. Keep an eye on your belongings if it means you have to leave them to help someone. Don't sacrifice your valuables for a trap! It's better to be safe than sorry, right?

Believe it or not, it doesn't always take a thief to make you lose something valuable, you can lose it all by yourself. Carelessness and forgetfulness can often lead to a habit of losing things. This may not be a big deal to you until it's your passport, or your iPod, or something else near and dear to your heart, and you're stranded without an ID, music, your photos, your journal or whatever it may be.

My own husband (before I knew him, I might add) once put his passport in the seat pocket in front of him on a flight from Switzerland to Amsterdam. When he went to board his connecting flight from Amsterdam back to the US, guess what he no longer had? That's right, his passport was still in the seat pocket, next to the vomit bag and the latest edition of *Sky Mall*. Fortunately for him, airline personnel were able to retrieve it and have it sent in the fastest golf cart in the airport to his gate, where he was literally the last one standing. He made it onto that flight with his passport in hand, but he was lucky that Amsterdam wasn't his final destination and that he hadn't left the airport, and more importantly that his previous flight was still in its gate when he realized what he'd forgotten.

This is where a mental check of your valuables (before you get off/on the plane/train/bus or perhaps when you leave your hotel/hostel) would be very handy. If it helps, make an actual list. For example, if everyday you want to carry with you your wallet, iPod, passport, and camera, then those are your four essentials to take with you (in the States mine are keys, wallet, phone, chapstick). Whenever I leave my house I run these four essentials through my head quickly to make sure I'll have everything I need. This is a good start, then I can add camera, bus pass, umbrella, or whatever I need according to where I am. Run it through your head on your way out the door so when you get across town to the Vatican you won't suddenly be caught without money or your camera! When you leave the restaurant where you just had lunch after visiting the Vatican, run through your list again to be sure you didn't leave any surprises for the servers.

Make another mental list for what you leave behind at your hotel, like your passport, extra money, iPod,

Kindle, extra memory cards for your camera, whatever it is that is most important. Every now and then double check and make sure it is all there, then you will always know where everything is. If you do this often enough, then when the time comes that something is actually missing (like my $100 emergency cash), you will definitely know when and where you last had possession of it. Knowing this information might not really help you other than determining that yes it was stolen or lost so you can stop looking for it.

Don't take more than you need to carry with you. Overpacking just causes painful shoulders from heavy purses or backpacks and more to lose if you are forgetful or if somehow you get robbed. It all comes back to being aware of both your surroundings and your belongings. Accidents and robberies can often be prevented; just don't leave your common sense at home!

Alcohol And Safety

I obviously cannot attempt to control your drinking habits by writing some words down in a book. I can, however, try to at least make you think twice about them.

What happens when you drink too much alcohol? You lose your capability of thinking rationally, perhaps you lose your sense of direction, and you might not even care at the moment. You may be used to these things and aware of how alcohol affects you personally, *in the States*. However, you may be surprised to learn that different climates, different elevations, even different alcohol can have a very different effect on you. This has the potential to put you in very bad situations.

Ladies, we've all heard the stories, there could be nothing worse than voluntarily putting yourself in a vulnerable position all because of alcohol. This type of situation *can* be avoided. This doesn't just go for women, either. Guys, you need to be just as aware. If you're old enough to be traveling abroad, you should be old enough to make good, responsible decisions, especially where your own safety is concerned.

Women Traveling Alone

As a solo female traveler for many years, I think I could probably write an entire book just about females traveling alone and attempting to stay safe in the process. Perhaps one day I will, but for now I am just going to mention one story that I hope every female who reads this keeps in mind as she travels.

This event took place in May 2013 in Kuala Lumpur, Malaysia. A female friend of mine was on vacation to Malaysia from Australia and was actually traveling with a male friend of hers. They attended a badminton tournament in a big, dirty stadium. It was broad daylight. She excused herself to go find the restroom, winding through food courts with plenty of people and eventually down some stairs and around a corner before she found it. Except for the fact that the lights were on, the restroom looked almost out of order. The doors to the stalls weren't even on hinges; they just leaned up against the stall walls. Being that this was likely her only option until returning to the hotel later, she chose the only stall with a semi-working door.

She was alone, but only for a moment. She actually didn't think twice when she heard someone else come in to the bathroom, although she did think it a bit strange that they chose the stall right next to hers. Just before she left the stall, she heard a strange noise and looked up. Now, what would you do if you actually saw a man (in full Malaysian army gear, no less) peeking over the stall wall, watching you do your business? She screamed as loudly and as angrily as she possibly could. Apparently this scared the guy so much that he actually fell from his post before he could manage to get to his feet and run out of there.

There is definitely a comical aspect to this story; however, there is also quite a lesson to be learned here. She had put herself in a very vulnerable situation without even realizing it. In my opinion, she also did the exact right thing by screaming as loudly as possible and attempting to attract any kind of attention to the situation. Luckily this man seemed to be nothing but a pervert and a coward, but if he had any malicious intent, she could have been in a very bad place. The imagination runs wild with "could-haves," but these are important things to think about. She is a beautiful girl, seemingly alone in a foreign place that she doesn't know, and here is a man preying on her just because he can. She is lucky that feeling violated was the extent of the harm in that experience.

Ladies, you can never play it too safe when it comes to your own safety. Unfortunately, some situations simply cannot be avoided. However, in situations like this one, if you keep safety as a priority, you may just trust your women's intuition or think to ask your male friend to wait outside the bathroom for you in a strange place. This is just one example out of an entire world of stories. Don't be ignorant or unassuming, and don't ever let your guard down when you sense you are in a sketchy place, especially if you are alone. It isn't worth it.

 *"Don't be ignorant or unassuming, and don't ever let your guard down when you sense you are in a sketchy place, especially if you are alone."*

Your personal safety abroad is not something that should be taken lightly, nor should you believe that "It will never happen to me." My goal is not to scare you, but to equip you with the information you have just read. Keep track of your belongings, don't fall victim to a distraction trap, don't offer yourself to bad situations, and keep your common sense about you. Time to take what you've learned from other people's mistakes and be a safety-smart traveler!

Chapter 7: Getting Money Abroad

There are many options when it comes to bringing or accessing money abroad:

- Bring plenty of US cash with you;

- Plan to use your ATM card;

- Plan to use your credit card;

- Get foreign money from your bank before you go.

If you notice, I did not mention Traveler's Checks. They are a cumbersome detail of the past that will probably soon be forgotten.

Bringing US Cash

You may want to do some research about whether or not your destination country accepts US dollars. This can be quite advantageous for you if it does. I know a lot of travelers who just bring a bundle of US cash with them, either planning to spend it normally or exchange it abroad. Exchanging cash abroad does cost money. Exchange rates are never quite in your favor, and you won't get a straight across exchange.

Using Your ATM Card

This is the option I am partial to, but I must preface this with the fact that I always bring about $100 emergency cash (in USD) to use or exchange later if necessary. Usually before I leave my arrival airport, I will stop at an ATM and pull out as much cash in the local currency that my bank in the US will allow me. This is about $300US. It does cost more to get money out of an ATM abroad than in the States, and then there are conversion fees, etc., and it can really add up. That is why I suggest pulling out the most allowed every time, to avoid paying the extra fees.

Now, for me the math is the hard part. I have never ever been good at math, and unfortunately I have a story to prove it. I once pulled the equivalent of $8 out of an ATM on my first day in a country where I wasn't yet familiar with the exchange rate. Somewhere I lost track of some zeros and my jet-lagged brain was loopy enough for me to make this mistake. Let this be a lesson to you to either do the math ahead of time when your brain is awake, or let someone who is good at math do it for you! It probably cost me $8 to get $8 out of that ATM, a complete waste of money. It was funny, yes, but unnecessary. I have since discovered an app called XE Currency that takes care of conversions for you. If you are also numerically challenged, you may benefit greatly from this free app!

Using Your Credit Card

This one usually goes hand in hand with using my ATM card for me. Be aware that most credit cards will charge you a 3% foreign transaction fee for every use of the card. This amount can also add up, but if you are using your credit card for small purchases, it does not add up very quickly. I usually try to figure out whether or not it's cheaper to pay the 3% fee than keep pulling money out of the ATM. Sometimes it's worth it, sometimes it isn't.

One thing I will warn against with credit cards is cash advance. Beware of using your credit card to get cash back from an ATM or other service, because depending on your card, a cash advance fee will probably cost you $30-40. I'd much rather pay the ATM fees. You may be advised to get a 4-number pin for your credit card, but you should also be fine without it. This pin will give you access to ATMs that you may as well avoid unless it's an emergency. To get a pin assigned to your credit card, just call the company and request one. If you plan to do this, don't wait until the last minute as it can take several business days.

Getting Foreign Currency From Your Bank

I don't think most people are even aware of this option, but it does exist. The only time I have actually done this was the first time I went to study abroad. I wasn't sure of how all the money worked yet, so I just went to my bank and ordered the currency of my choice. It was a straight across exchange, so there were no fees involved whatsoever, and I was prepared before I even stepped on the plane. If you opt to do this, make sure you give your bank enough to time order your currency if it is not something mainstream like Euros or Pounds, etc. because they won't have it on hand to exchange for you.

It will only last you so long, of course, and then you will still need to get money out of the ATM or use a credit card, but it could save some stress right at the beginning of your trip.

Finally, there is the option of prepaid cash cards. I have a friend who has used these in the past and she seemed to like them, but I can't say much about them because I have never used one. You can always contact your bank if you are interested in more information about cash cards, I just personally can't recommend using them.

Contact Your Banks

There is one rule above all others that you would do well to follow, regardless of how you plan to get money abroad: let your banks know that you are taking your

ATM and credit cards abroad! If you don't do this, chances are very high that your bank will red flag your card and either freeze it or shut down your account entirely after your first transaction. Even if this account freeze is temporary, it is a major inconvenience. If this happens, not only will you not be able to get any money out of that account, but you will also need to figure out a way to get in contact with your bank in the US, reactivate your account, and perhaps arrange to receive a new card in the mail because yours is now deactivated. The mail? While traveling? Yes, this is why you should avoid the situation completely. It is often the last thing I do in the airport before boarding my flight abroad, but I always make a point to do it. Call the number on the back of your card (all the cards you are bringing) and advise your bank(s) of your travels.

"There is one rule above all others that you would do well to follow... let your banks know that you are taking your ATM and credit cards abroad!"

Have A Backup Plan

That brings up another point: Have a backup plan. If you only bring one source of money abroad with you (one ATM or credit card or whatever it might be) what sort of trouble will you be in if you misplace it or if the bank freezes it? Let's not go there. Make sure you bring at least two sources of plastic access to your accounts, even if one is for emergencies only. Here's another tip: don't pack them in the same place. If you keep both or all of your cards in one wallet and then lose it, you will be no better off than you would had you only brought one card. Keep secret stashes of these important things so that you can be as prepared as possible for anything.

Lastly, if you have a choice of credit cards to bring abroad, try to bring either a Visa or MasterCard. Those are the most-accepted credit cards worldwide. You might have trouble if you try to bring a Discover or American Express; you may not be able to use them at all depending on where you go. If you have a card with a chip in it, definitely bring that, and if your card does not have a chip, try contacting your bank to see if they offer cards with a chip. It is a system that hasn't quite hit the US, but rather than swiping cards, many countries insert them just far enough to read the chip and that's all it takes for a transaction.

You may also want to bring a specific coin purse or pocket of some sort, as many countries use more coins than we do in the US. However you decide to bring your money, whether it's cash or credit, be sure to keep track of it, stash it in different places, and tell your bank(s) you're leaving.

Chapter 8: Making It Work Abroad

Cell Phones

Many travelers opt to have a fully-functioning cell phone abroad. Even for short periods of travel, a cell phone can come in handy for many reasons. There are a couple of options for what cell phones you can use abroad:

- Unlock and use your US smartphone (if possible); or,

- Use any cell phone that is SIM-capable (you may need to purchase this abroad).

Here is how it works. In the US, many of us are bound to contracts through one carrier. We pay monthly and receive the service we pay for. However, in many foreign countries there are no contracts, just SIM cards. A SIM card is a tiny data card that fits somewhere into your phone. SIM stands for Subscriber Identity Module. Basically, a SIM card is your service, your cell phone carrier, your phone number, everything.

Unbeknownst to many, your US smartphone may be SIM-capable. Find out by contacting your cellular service provider and asking that they unlock your phone for use abroad. At time of publishing, the White House was trying to require wireless carriers to unlock all mobile devices, which would be wonderfully convenient for more than just the travel community. However, we'll have to see what happens with that. Getting your cell phone unlocked should not cost you anything. This will "unlock" the international SIM capability on your phone so that you can use your phone with a SIM in a foreign country. It does not affect the function of your phone in the US, nor does it affect your service in the US (which we covered in Chapter 5). It just allows you to take your beloved smartphone and use it abroad rather than having to purchase some other phone (heaven forbid) that is SIM capable.

The easiest way to unlock your phone is to call your cell phone provider's customer service number and talk to the right person. Don't wait until the last minute to do this, as some companies claim that it may take a few days to grant your request. Once your phone is unlocked, you can take it abroad and use it. If you don't have a smartphone that is SIM-capable, don't worry. You can always purchase a cell phone abroad that will work with any SIM card.

How To Get A SIM Card Abroad

Chances are there will be several competing cell phone service providers in your destination country, much like there are in the US. You may want to ask around or perhaps do a bit of research to find out which one you should choose. Once you decide, find a cell phone store (these are usually very easy to find) that carries SIM cards for that provider and purchase a SIM. You may need your passport when purchasing a SIM, so be prepared. The cost for just a SIM card could be anywhere around $5-20, give or take a bit, depending on the country.

The next step is to put some credit on your SIM card so you can actually use your phone. If you aren't sure where to look, ask for help, but there should be cards by your service provider with varying amounts of credit on them. These are often called recharge cards. You pay for it right there in the store. To apply the credit you just purchased onto your SIM, follow the instructions on the card. This usually consists of dialing a given number and going through the automated instructions, which will prompt you to enter a scratch-off code that you will find on your card. These recharge cards are pay-as-you-go, so you can repeat the recharge process as often as you need, no contracts necessary.

WARNING: If you are in a country with a foreign language, you may want to ask for help doing this automated process, because you certainly don't want to mess it up!

If you will be traveling in multiple countries, it may be cheaper to buy local SIM cards for each country than to pay the international rates of your first destination country's SIM card. You may also find that different countries use different providers, which could result in you not finding your specific provider. Therefore, you may want to be sure to stock up on credit before you leave the country if you opt not to get a new SIM in the next country.

In the past when I have lived abroad, I almost always had a cell phone. The least I paid was about $10 for a phone (a very basic dumb phone) and probably $5-10 for a SIM card in Brazil. Obviously that phone wasn't anything fancy, but it made calls and sent text messages, which was all I needed. If these things are important to you, then you can get them easily and inexpensively.

If you also want to have access to Internet on your phone, then you have a couple of options: either unlock and get a SIM for a smartphone that is Internet-capable, or bring a device that has Wi-Fi capabilities for use with Wi-Fi hotspots. It seems to make the most sense to just use one device for everything, but if you don't have one or won't need Internet that much, using Wi-Fi when it's available is another option.

Must-Have Travel Apps

As travelers in this day and age, we can stay connected to the world at our fingertips through our mobile devices. There are so many tools we can use to help us on our way that it would be a shame not to take advantage of them. Especially when they help save you time and money, which most of these apps have the potential to do. New apps are developed every day, so always be on the lookout for great new ideas. I'm going to share with you some of today's travel apps that I have found to be super helpful. You can search for them by name and download all of them for free in your app store:

- **Hostelworld:** Who doesn't need a hostel-booking engine at their fingertips? This app is one of my go-to accommodation providers when I am on the road. You can use it to search hostels, hotels, bed & breakfasts, apartments, and even campgrounds all over the world. Hostelworld is a long-trusted organization offering competitive prices, so I feel comfortable booking with them and I know I am always getting a deal.

- **Airbnb:** If you prefer off the beaten path places to stay, or perhaps boutique hotels or even entire houses to rent, Airbnb would be a good app for you. It is a booking engine that offers many lodging options that mainstream booking engines do not have access to. Each listing includes a profile about the person or people who own the places, complete with reviews and references. The booking fees are higher with Airbnb, but the options are usually more unique.

- **TripAdvisor:** Most of you have probably heard of this organization because they are quite a presence in the travel community. In fact, they claim to be the "world's largest travel site" offering over 100 million reviews, photos, and more, all provided by travelers. It is a great way to find out what people have to say about a certain hotel, restaurant, or activity that you are considering, just keep in mind you may not have the same preferences as many travelers who leave reviews.

- **Booking.com:** The only hotel-booking engine you need. It offers the best deals, a huge selection, photos, reviews, and everything you need to make a decision about where to stay. Bookings go through within minutes, so don't be afraid to step away from reception and use it if it will save you some money! (Like we did in Chapter 3)

- **Free Wi-Fi Finder:** Wherever you are in the world, you can use this app to find free wi-fi. It even works when you are offline, through some magic with "network triangulation" and GPS capabilities. If you do not have a data plan on your cell phone while you are abroad, most apps on your phone are only accessible with wi-fi, so this app could really come in handy for you.

- **GateGuru:** Here is where apps get really magical. Through GateGuru you can access real-time flight statuses for thousands of airports worldwide. Departures, arrivals, delays, cancellations, it's all there. You can even find out what restaurants and shops there are in your terminal! Now if that isn't genius, I don't know what is. This is the only app that provides these services, so be sure to download it before you head out for your long day of transit.

- **Wikihood:** This app organizes the information in Wikipedia by location. Meaning, you can search a destination and soon you will see what points of interest are around you, what others find interesting in that place, how to get to a specific location by map, any important history related to that place, and much more. It is basically a guidebook come to life, and there are customization options and offline options for a small fee, but the regular app is free. To have all that information at your fingertips is like having a tour guide in your pocket. Leave the guidebook at home!

- **XE Currency:** I mentioned this one in Chapter 7 with my embarassing miscalculation at the ATM. Never again will this happen to me, because I have XE Currency. Tell it to convert any amount of currency into any other currency and it will give you exact, up-to-date (yes, up-to-date exchange rate) calculations, saving you the headache of wasting the brain power to figure it out. For the numerically challenged, don't leave this one at home!

Visa Issues

In Chapter 1 I mentioned the possibility of having to show proof of onward travel when crossing land borders. This is a requirement to enter some countries. If you do not have it, you may be forced to get it in order to enter the country. If this happens to you, there is an inexpensive way around it. If you truly have no idea how long you plan to stay or by what manner you will be leaving, simply purchase a bus ticket out of the country to the nearest town for some future date, even a few days later. This shouldn't be too difficult given the fact that you will be at a border crossing. If you end up using the ticket, great, if you make another plan, then just consider it part of your visa fee and forget about it. I've never actually had to do this, but that could very well have been dependent on the mood of the immigration officers on the days I've crossed land borders. It's good to have a plan, just in case.

I would highly recommend that you do not stay longer than your allotted time as a visitor in any given country (the amount of days varies by country and will be noted on your passport entry stamp). Depending on the country, the rules can be pretty strict. If you overstay your welcome, sometimes you can get away without any problems, other times you may not be so lucky. I have overstayed my visa limit twice, and I happened to get lucky both times, but I also have horror stories about those times and I won't do it again. I don't want anyone to think it's okay. I wouldn't want to find out what happens when travelers aren't so lucky. Actually I'm really curious, I just don't want to be the one to find out *personally.*

"I would highly recommend that you do not stay longer than your allotted time as a visitor in any given country."

Many countries have very loose visa regulations and only require that you leave the country every three months for at least 72 hours. Such are the regulations in Costa Rica. When I lived there, our student visas never went through (who knows why, Tico time?), but it didn't matter. We happily traveled to Nicaragua or Panama for several days whenever our three-month periods were nearing an end. Some countries aren't so simple. Plan ahead, or at least have a *really* good Plan B for the moment you attempt to leave the country and the authorities stop you because your visa has expired....

Travel Insurance

I always recommend that travelers have some sort of insurance coverage. This can come in more than one way. Some credit cards will cover a number of things like baggage delay, flight delay, and even rental car insurance. Keep in mind, you have to buy your plane ticket or rent your car with that credit card if you want to have the coverage. This is a money-saving way to go about being covered by insurance, because it doesn't cost you anything extra. Look over your credit card policy to see what it includes, and then you can make a decision about whether or not you need insurance coverage.

What To Look For In Travel Insurance Coverage

There are several things I specifically require for myself when I buy travel insurance:

- **Trip Cancellation (pre-departure) and Trip Interruption (post-departure):** If for any (covered) reason you have to cancel your trip *before* you leave, Trip Cancellation will cover your payments and deposits that you made pre-departure. If for any (covered) reason you cannot continue your trip *after* you've started, Trip Interruption will cover any non-refundable trip costs once you have begun your trip.

- **Travel Delay:** If your travel (on a main carrier) is delayed by a certain number of hours (for a covered reason) you would be entitled to coverage for meals, accommodations if necessary, and any non-refundable and unused deposits paid.

- **Baggage Delay coverage:** This will vary by how many hours your luggage can be late before insurance kicks in. This insurance may also only cover certain items (toiletries, a change of clothing, etc.) so make sure you are aware of what will be covered before you go on a shopping spree.

- **Lost Baggage coverage:** This covers the amount your luggage is worth if and when the airline actually loses it for good. Let's hope you won't need this one, but it's great to have just in case.

- **Accidental Death (Common Carrier or Flight):** For those without life insurance. I know no one wants to think about this, but in the worst-case scenario, you will be covered if your plane or train or bus crashes. (Just make sure to tell someone about your policy *before* you go...)

- **Medical Evacuation:** In case something happens to you and you can't get proper medical treatment where you are, this will pay for you to get transferred to somewhere with adequate medical care. (Things to think about when you're traveling in the Third World).

- **Medical:** Pay attention to the small print on your policy, generally medical coverage up to a certain amount is included for the first 30 days or so. If your trip will be longer than 30 days, you can purchase extra medical coverage. Many countries have great, affordable access to health care so you may not even need this coverage. However, you never know what could happen, and it's only costing you a few dollars to be covered.

- **Extreme Sports:** Lastly, there is sometimes an option to add extreme sport coverage (for an extra fee) to your policy. If you know you will be participating in extreme sports (sky-diving, white-water rafting, canyoning, ziplining, etc.), you may want this coverage for extra peace of mind.

Where should you get travel insurance? I highly recommend InsureMyTrip.com. You can view and compare several policies through several different providers. I have always purchased my travel insurance through InsureMyTrip, and I have always been satisfied with my policies and providers. In fact, I actually filed a Trip Interruption claim once after that major problem I went through in Brazil, and it was honored. This was a huge relief for me since I had several deposits and even a flight that were non-refundable and unused. That was through an American Express policy I had purchased through InsureMyTrip, and I definitely highly recommend them. You can also find great travel insurance packages through World Nomads. Start with those two companies; you will find what you need.

Adapters And Converters

One thing to keep in mind when you will be traveling abroad is the type of outlets you will be faced with in your destination country(ies). It is a good idea to bring a universal adapter with you. This will allow you to use any type of outlet you might come across. Now, being able to plug in to any outlet is one thing, but voltage and conversion is a completely different factor that you should consider. Many girls have gone abroad and lost their hair dryers on the first surge of electricity. Likewise, many guys have lost their razors to this unfortunate event. Voltage differences can be a big bummer if you don't plan accordingly.

Consider getting an adapter that also converts voltage to be spared from the voltage trap. You should buy this in the US prior to your departure for three reasons:

- You know you'll be able to find the exact product you need with the appropriate outlets;

- Electronics in the US are cheaper than many places abroad;

- You want to be prepared.

If you aren't sure what kind of outlets are used in your destination country, look it up online. Many countries use the same two-prong outlets as the US, and that makes it simple. However, many others have all kinds of shapes and sizes of outlets, so if you want to be able to use your electronics, it may be wise to look it up before you go.

If you are an Apple person, you will be delighted to hear that your plug that came with your iPhone or MacBook has a converter in it (that little white box). So you should be able to plug it in via your adapter without worry.

Chapter 9: Study Abroad

Now that you have read enough to prepare yourself for a great trip, it's time to put what you've learned into action. If you are in college, studying abroad is a great option for you, and even if you aren't in college, you don't have to be a current student to be eligible. The way I really got my start was through studying abroad. I had been on mission trips to Mexico several times throughout high school, but the first time I really traveled abroad was when I joined a program at age 18 and went to Costa Rica to study Spanish. When I went to college, my family and I had just come off of a year as hosts to a German foreign exchange student. I still think of her as my sister today. She gave me some advice before she left to go home to Germany. She said, "Wherever you go, go for an entire year, don't even think twice about it."

"Wherever you go, go for an entire year, don't even think twice about it."

During my freshman orientation at college we had these breakout sessions where we could go learn about different clubs and opportunities through the university, and I went to the study abroad session. It was for a program called USAC (University Studies Abroad Consortium), which just happened to be headquartered at my school, but has a number of participating universities all throughout the US. I remember looking around the room with complete and utter envy at all the raised hands when the presenter asked, "How many of you have studied abroad before?" I'm not even quite sure where the urge came from to follow through with it so early in my college career, but I spent that year applying to go for a year abroad in Costa Rica with USAC. In most college programs, you have to be at least a sophomore to study abroad. So when I was a sophomore in college, I left.

That was just the first time, and just the beginning for me. I can only think back and reflect on it as complete fate that I went abroad that year, because traveling has shaped me into who I was meant to be all along. After that first year in Costa Rica, I came back and applied to spend another year with USAC in Italy. I have always said that there is so much more that you can learn from traveling the world than from being in a classroom. Sure, I ended up with a degree after five travel-filled years of college, which I like to refer to as "the scenic route." However, what I really gained was the ability to grow everyday, to challenge myself, to make important decisions on my own, to see the world through someone else's eyes, to speak multiple languages, to feel completely comfortable in a completely foreign culture, to have an open mind, to believe in myself, to stand up for myself, to know what I stand for, to know what I want in life, and to understand that I need to encourage others to learn these same things for themselves, among many, many other things.

I can't say enough about studying abroad. I have done it three times, to three countries with three different foreign languages, on three different continents. These were three of the best experiences of my life. I am planning to go again and again to continue learning foreign languages whenever I can make it work.

I have technically spent more time studying abroad than traveling abroad, and there is something really special about it that you can't quite get when you are just traveling. I always had a sense of belonging, of friendship, of structure, and of purpose in my life during those times of study abroad. When I have been just traveling, there is always the next place, the next country, the next adventure, the next friends to look forward to, and it is just a completely different kind of structure when you are a nomad. Even if you find yourself in one place for a while, which I have, it still feels different from taking classes, living in and traveling from one place, and having the same friends for months.

I'm not saying that simply traveling is worse in any way; I'm just saying it's really different. In my life, there are no glory days of the past, I don't see my study abroad experiences like that. But I do see them as unmatched opportunities for students to get abroad, get educated by the world rather than a classroom, and get bitten by the travel bug that will hopefully leave them yearning for more. Study abroad is a structured, organized, easy-to-accept invitation, a simple gateway to the world.

If you are considering studying abroad even the littlest bit, you must go, and go for an entire year. Don't think twice about it; you won't regret it.

Conclusion

When my year in Costa Rica came to an end, and after I had already extended my flight so I could stay for one more month, I had no choice but to return home to the US. I remember staring out the window at those same, now familiar, beautiful, green mountains with tears on my face on the flight back. I like to say that I took that flight "kicking and screaming," figuratively speaking of course, but it was definitely against my will. I had a secret plan to move back in six months to the country I had grown to love so deeply. When "life" kicked back in, my ambitions changed and instead of going back to Costa Rica, I ended up studying Italian in Italy, a change of plans which I do not regret one bit. I was hooked. Addicted to travel. Addicted to the world that I had learned was so much bigger than the country I grew up in.

There is so much out there to be seen, learned, explored, and experienced in a way that you simply must do it yourself. *It won't always be rainbows and butterflies, but it will always be worth it.* Both my highest highs and lowest lows have been while I've been somewhere out in the world, alone. I believe life starts at the edge of your comfort zone. It makes every experience not only more challenging but also more rewarding, and you've no choice but to learn and grow as a person. Get out, meet the world, and let it change you and your perspective for the better.

Thank You!

I would like to personally thank you for reading this book. I hope you have been inspired or learned something that will help you on your way to get out and explore the world.

I would love it if you would take a moment to offer any feedback or comments about the book on my website at thebudgetmindedtraveler.com/book, and while you're there check out my blog where I post articles about all sorts of travel tips much like the ones here.

If you feel that someone else would appreciate the information in this book, please tell them about it. This country could really benefit from a few more world travelers.

Finally, I'd love to connect with you! Please "like" and follow The Budget-Minded Traveler page on Facebook at facebook.com/thebudgetmindedtraveler and leave a comment, or follow me on Twitter (@budgetmtraveler). Thank you so much and happy travels!

Bonus Alert! Blog Sneak Peeks

www.TheBudgetMindedTraveler.com/blog

I'd love for you to visit and subscribe to my blog, especially if you enjoy articles like the ones to follow in this sneak peek section!

What Stands Between You And Your Wishes To Travel The World?

Published 8/15/13

Are your job and finances standing between you and travel?

It doesn't matter if you have visited foreign countries before or not; world travel is in the face of us all everyday. We are all on Facebook, seeing the statuses of our friends who are in some exotic location posting photos that you'd almost rather not look at. Or perhaps you have friends who are planning their honeymoons or yearly trips abroad, or whatever it may be. Travel is present in our lives whether we take part in it or not, and I have a feeling that if you're reading this, you are one who would like to take part.

Just what you wanted to see while you're "stuck" at work, right?

For many, there seems to be this minor detail we call "work" that may be the biggest obstacle that stands between you and traveling the world. The other obstacle would most likely be money, as for some it is seemingly impossible to save. When I talk to people who wish they could travel more, the biggest reasons why they can't are their jobs and their finances.

So what can be done about these two rather large obstacles? I truly believe there is a somewhat simple, straightforward answer to this question, and it lies in your priorities.

Are your priorities in the right order?

I'm not going to tell you what you should and shouldn't spend your money on, or that you should quit your job right now and buy a plane ticket. That is not for me to say, and those decisions must be made responsibly in all of our lives. What I do know, and the biggest thing I've noticed when talking with most people who wish they could travel more, is that our lives reflect our priorities. Priorities can change as often as life throws changes at us, but it is how we handle them that determines our lifestyles.

"...our lives reflect our priorities..."

I touched on this a bit in my first blog post, but I'm going to elaborate a little more in hopes that it will at least encourage you to think about your priorities. The best way I can share this with you is by using my own experience, so I'm going to show you what my work and money priorities look like, because maintaining control of both of these obstacles is what allows me to keep travel as a high priority in my life (and actually act on it).

How I prioritize travel and get over the obstacles of work and money.

Ever since I first studied abroad in Costa Rica at age 18, I have always had my next international trip formulating in my mind until it becomes a plan and I eventually get on a plane. This is something I simply must do. To me this has meant two things: one, I need to make enough money to make that trip happen; and two, I need to have a job that I can easily leave to make that trip happen. This is my lifestyle when it comes to money and work. Travel is obviously a very high priority. I simply find ways to make it happen because I want it badly enough.

Work

- I have never had a job that I felt prevented me from sticking to my travel plans. I would never *take* a job that prevented me from

119
www.TheBudgetMindedTraveler.com

traveling. If a company wants too much from me and won't allow me the time off that I need, truly need every year to feel like I am living my life the way I need to, then that company isn't worth my time. There are other jobs.

- I was "lucky" enough to work in seasonal positions for many years, allowing me to come and go conveniently. The service industry (serving in restaurants) was great for this because really, no one cares when you leave and there are plenty of people to fill your position. I couldn't handle the service industry forever, so I am now self-employed, which is both terrifying and liberating, but most of all it allows me to have complete control over my schedule.

- I tried having a permanent position (working for someone else) once. It lasted for one year and simply didn't suit me. If work was my highest priority or if I was passionate about that job, I may have thought differently, but that just wasn't the case, so I left that job because it didn't reflect my priorities.

Money

- If the amount of money I need for something is not in my bank account, I can't afford it. Period.

- Monthly payments take away from our travel fund. We keep them to a minimum.

- Yes, we use credit cards but we pay them off every month. I have never taken out a loan, nor am I in debt. Without this weight on my shoulders, I am free to save money for traveling. If you are in debt, make it your number one priority to get out, as quickly as possible (that probably goes without saying).

- I have a '94 Toyota Pickup that is completely paid off. My husband owns a '97 Subaru that is completely paid off. We love our old cars, especially because together we have $0/mo in car payments (and Toyotas and Subarus last a long time!). If and when the time comes to buy a "new" car, we will purchase a used car in full in order to avoid a monthly payment. New cars are completely overrated.

- There are so many ways we save money: buying a six pack of beer at the store instead of going downtown for one drink at the same price; participating in clothing swaps (super fun by the way) instead of going shopping for myself when I don't really *need* new clothes; inviting friends over for a BBQ instead of going out for dinner; thinking twice before purchasing things. We deem a *lot* of things "unnecessary spending" and decide to save instead of spend. The amount we save in a year just by thinking about our spending is probably enough to buy a plane ticket to Europe.

- If we are on a tight budget and planning a trip (like we are currently), prioritizing money is a mind game. Would I rather go out to dinner with my husband tonight or in six weeks when we're in Europe? To the grocery store we go to cook dinner at home...

Do you *really* want to travel?

The decisions you make about your job and your finances should reflect your priorities. What is most important to you? How bad do you want to take that trip you have only dreamed about?

How are *your* priorities preventing you from seeing the world? If you want to travel the world, you will. Period. If you want it badly enough, you *will* find a way. That goes for anything in life. Your travel priority will make its way up your list until it is close enough to reach the top, and then you can actually start to plan a trip. Once you do it the first time, it is much easier to do it a second, third, and many more times. If it turns out that you really enjoy traveling like I do, it is likely that it will remain close to the top of your priority list, and you will simply find ways to get over the obstacles and make it happen.

"If you want it badly enough, you *will* find a way."

What To Do When The Travel Bug Bites

(And You Can't Leave Yet)

Published 7/11/13

TBA- A Very Real Syndrome

It doesn't matter that I've been out of the country twice already this year, I am having a serious case of TBA these days. TBA stands for Travel Bug Anxiety. No, you probably won't find any real definition for it since I made it up, but that is exactly what is getting to me. The travel bug is biting, hard. Maybe you have experienced this at some point? (If not yet, you will). You get so antsy that you can't concentrate, you find yourself wanting to cry when you look at photos from abroad, you stare at the map on your wall for entirely too long, you definitely can't get any work done, and you pace the house feeling like you're about to explode, or break down, or something, all because you can't get your mind off of traveling. This, my friends, is TBA.

Okay, I Have Self-Diagnosed, Now What?

There were three specific things that I did over the weekend that really helped bring my temperature down from TBA. I don't think anything but setting foot abroad will actually make it go away, but these things helped enough that I would recommend anyone suffering from TBA should try them out:

- Read a really good book that takes place somewhere far away.

- Give yourself a taste of where you are dying to go.

- Make a plan to get there (preferably within the next six months).

The place I'm dying to go right now is Europe.

I didn't realize it when I picked up *The Lost Symbol* by Dan Brown, but I was definitely headed to Washington D.C. for the weekend, even though I never left Montana. I know, Washington D.C. doesn't seem like all that far away (and it's definitely not Europe), but this book incorporated a lot of history and architecture, specifically European, which was a great escape for me. It was a good enough read that I was finished with it in three days, and I felt like I had just experienced a great adventure. I LOVE books that have this effect, and if you have any to recommend, please do so. Reading the book was the first step to somewhat alleviating my TBA.

My cravings for Europe have been so intense lately that I simply needed to give myself a taste, literally, of Europe. My go-to is Italian cuisine since I have lived there twice and prefer it over pretty much everything else. I wanted to do something I would normally only do in Italy. My husband joined me in my little venture. We started by walking (not driving, because I wouldn't do that in Italy), to a nearby coffee shop, where I proceeded to order a cappuccino. I never order these in the States, but I ALWAYS order them in Italy because they are so simply delicious. I always fear that baristas in the US don't know how to make a proper cappuccino; it's very hit or miss entirely. Luckily for me, the barista at our local coffee shop did a great job, although it was huge; it must have been 16 oz., which was entirely too big for me at 5pm (but I didn't complain). We sat outside on a bench with a horrible view of an alley parking lot, but I was imagining old buildings and piazzas, trying to do my best with what I had. (If I sound crazy now, you just wait until you start traveling). We talked about our travel options, and slowly started formulating a plan to get to Europe (twice, I might add). I felt better after having just talked about it over a cappuccino. (Not entirely better, but better).

After the cappuccino, we walked to a market that actually has a lot of specialty Italian food (right in my neighborhood. Coincidence? More like destiny). We had decided against going out to eat and instead splurged on some tasty Italian food and wine. Then we walked home, put on some traditional Italian music (gotta love Pandora), and proceeded to cook up a fancy, simply delicious meal. My brother joined us, which seemed very fitting since we almost always travel to Europe with him. After we enjoyed our caprese antipasto and pesto pasta, we took our wine out to our front steps and attempted to people watch, much like we would do in Italy. It wasn't quite the same, but then again, we really were in Montana and it was the best we could do. We had a great time, and I concluded that after both reading the book and spending an "evening in Italy," I did feel a lot better. Until I have a plane ticket in hand, this method will have to suffice. We decided we wouldn't stop with Italy, but that we would continue on a tour of Europe for the weeks to come. Next stop, Deutschland!

What Would You Do?

If you haven't traveled at all or very much, you may think I'm talking crazy. However, once you start to explore the world of travel, you will eventually have a case of TBA yourself. I know there are those of you out there who can relate to my TBA experience. The question is, since we know there is "no known antidote" for the travel bug, what do we do about it? I really think the only way I will make this specific case of TBA go away is by actually getting on a plane to Europe, but that won't happen for a few months. I have just shared some things I did to help quell the symptoms, and now I want to hear from you. How do we help ourselves keep TBA to a minimum while we are still Stateside?

My Travel Bucket List

_____

_____

_____

_____

_____

_____

_____

_____

_____

_____

_____

_____

_____

Notes

_____

_____

_____

_____

_____

_____

_____

_____

_____

_____

_____

_____

_____

_____

Notes